ideas • ingenuity • passion • creativity • inventiveness • inspiration

Everything in life starts as an idea. Something crosses your mind, vagrant and casual, maybe as a little breeze that stirs the hollyhocks outside your window. If you entertain the idea for a moment, it seems to leave a deposit in your brain cells which makes it easy for the thought to come again.

Excerpt from Leaves from Lantern Lane, Nellie McClung, 1936

1

Acknowledgements

Canadian Women Invent! is blessed with many friends who contributed to the project in countless numbers of ways. Thank you to Lisa Pleau for believing from the beginning, Claire Watson Garcia, Karen Ketcheson, John Vollmer, Joanne De Laurentiis, and Charlie Coffey for their mentoring, care and unflagging positive energy, Johanna Skelly, herself an innovator, artist, and contributor to the book, for her constant support and encouragement, Plum Johnson who reminded us always of the inventor's journey, David Scopick and Michel Blondeau for their wealth of technical knowledge, Bill Gulletson for his financial guidance, Richard Garvin for his creative contributions, Stephen Mitchell for his excellent editorial support. Appreciation is extended to the Bata Shoe Museum (Toronto) for providing Inventive Women Inc. access to the museum's collection of Northern artifacts.

Inventive Women Inc. thanks Doreen Dotto for her steadfast commitment and contribution, and her children Max and Jackson for their input as junior advisors to the project. Ron, Emily and Michael Wood comprised a cheering section that encouraged the project along. Ron's photography has enriched the book immeasurably. Thank you. And to the inventors whose inspiring contributions fuelled this project, thank you for the impressive heritage that you've allowed Inventive Women Inc. to showcase.

Annie Wood

Curiosity about women's achievements as agents of technological change inspired Annie to start Inventive Women Inc. Previously, she was one of the founders of the Canadian children's publishing company, Kids Can Press. Many of today's much loved children's book authors and illustrators were first published by Annie. She co-authored (with Ian Wallace) the children's book classic *The Sandwich*. The book has been in print for twenty-six years.

Fani Evagelou

Canadian Women Invent! is Fani's first book. As contributing writer and researcher, Fani enjoyed the opportunity to learn about the achievements of our inventive women. She also greatly enjoyed being a part of the Inventive Women Inc. team. She thanks Annie for the opportunity to participate in this special endeavour, and hopes that it has a lasting impact in the sense that it inspires Canadians of all ages to be inventive and innovative.

Catherine Farquharson

Of course there are women inventors. But naming them was a different story all together for Catherine Farquharson. The need to find out was enough to pull Catherine to this project. She is currently studying Journalism at Ryerson University, and is proud to say she can name not one, but many women inventors.

Alex Hadjiantoniou

This is Alex's debut as a book illustrator. He started his career as a storyboard artist for television commercials with companies such as HMV and Toshiba. Presently, Alex is studying illustration at the Ontario College of Art and Design.

Canadian Women
Invent!

ideas · ingenuity · passion · creativity · inventiveness · inspiration

Annie Wood

with Fani Evagelou and Catherine Farquharson

Illustrated by Alex Hadjiantoniou

To innovation!

We gratefully acknowledge the financial support of the Government of Canada through the Millennium Partnership Program, and the Canadian Studies Program (Department of Canadian Heritage).

Dedications

A.W. – To Emily, Michael and Ron, with gratitude.
F.E. – I'd like to thank Trinity for picking me up when I fall down.

Published in Canada by Inventive Women Inc.
401 Richmond Street West, Suite 358
Toronto, Ontario, Canada, M5V 3A8
info@inventivewomen.com
www.inventivewomen.com
www.inventivekids.com

Canadian Catalogue in Publication Data

Wood, Annie
Evagelou, Fani
Farquharson, Catherine
Canadian Women Invent!

Includes Index.
ISBN 0-9689651-0-5
1. Women Inventors - Biography - Juvenile Literature
2. Inventions - History - Juvenile Literature
3. Women - Canada - History - 20th Century

Editing by Emily Wood, Johanna Skelly, Cathy Lofgreen
Research by Fani Evagelou, Rebecca Burton, Kirstie McCallum
Photography by Ron Wood, Heartline Pictures Inc., Toronto
Design by Inventive Women Inc.
Printed in Toronto by F.W. Barrett Company

Photo Credits:
page 17, Margaret Duley, Centre for Newfoundland Studies Archives (Alison Feder, MF - 213), Memorial University of Newfoundland, St. John's, Newfoundland
page 39, "Queen of the Hurricanes" (MG 31 K 7, vol. 16, file 7, National Archives of Canada c146539)
page 68, Great Northern Arts Festival website, www.greatart.nt.ca

Contents

ideas • ingenuity • passion • creativity • inventiveness • inspiration

Foreword

Do women invent?
Just take a look around!

Whether you are relaxing in your living room, studying at school, working at your office, or shopping in a store, inventions by women are every-where. From the tasty chocolate chip cookie to advanced computer programming, products and processes invented by women worldwide are an important part of everyone's lives.

This book begins to tell the impressive story of Canada's remarkable female inventors and innovators. Their ideas have changed the way we live and have become a rich part of our national heritage. Our researchers discovered inventive Canadian women at work from coast to coast – in every province and territory, in every industry, and in every walk of life. They can be found in high-tech manufacturing firms, in retail shops, in universities, in homes, in high schools, at the bottom of deep mine shafts, and in orbit high above the earth. In a single word, they are everywhere.

We owe a huge debt to every inventor and innovator who took the time to tell the story of her work, and who had the candour to share her personal story as well. We are particularly grateful to the women working in technical areas who had the patience to help non-experts grasp complex concepts and subject matter.

In addition to researching and interviewing active inventors and innovators, we have combed Canada's historical books and records to learn about women from our past. In some cases, all that remains of their work is a footnote, or the record of a patent application. We can only imagine the stories of struggle and triumph that lie behind some of these brief entries.

You will notice that all the female inventors in this book are problem-solvers. Some women solved problems that were connected to their occupations. While others found creative solutions to challenges they experienced in their daily lives. The student inventors featured in the book used a fresh "why not" approach to finding solutions to environ-mental problems in their communities. Through innovative science fair

Technology is the science and art of making and using things, by turning the materials of the natural world into tools and machines.

An invention is any new thing created which improves the way something is done, or introduces a new way of doing things. Inventions can be intentional or accidental, practical or fun!

Innovations are changes to things that already exist.

projects, these young women were able to fine-tune their scientific and inventive skills, and develop technologies that may eventually rid the earth of pollutants.

Many of the inventions you will read about are the result of dynamic research being carried out at universities and research centres across the country by specialists in all fields. Some of the inventions are the first of their kind, while others have advanced existing technologies and processes. In each case, the invention has benefited others by making the world healthier and more enjoyable.

The idea for the Inventive Women project began several years ago with a query from a curious young student who wanted to know if women invented. When she and I sought the answer to that question, we discovered surprisingly few resources on female inventors. This book is part of an attempt to begin to fill that void, but it is only a beginning. It offers a brief introduction to the work of the women we have featured. And it only scratches the surface of literally thousands of examples of invention and innovation by Canadian women.

We hope you will take the time to find out more about the inventions, projects, and people mentioned here. We also hope you will be on the lookout for inventive women at work in your own local community or neighbourhood – or even in your own family! Most of all, we hope this book will be an inspiration to young women of today who are eager to put their own inventive ideas into gear. Canada's new generation of female inventors and innovators now have dynamic role models to help them succeed.

Annie Wood, Inventive Women Inc.

Inventors are people who can see new needs, find ways of meeting them, and see opportunity and value in accidental discoveries.

Scientists are researchers who use experiments and scientific testing to discover new laws and principles of nature.

Engineers are trained in science, mathematics, and industrial processes. Their training allows them to use their knowledge to convert raw materials and power sources into needed products and services. Engineers usually work in teams to invent a new device, method, or process.

Who Are They?

Some of the first technological inventions may not seem like much to us now, like the digging stick, which pre-historic people used for finding food and for planting seeds. But each and every invention was an important technology at the time and helped us to evolve into the people we are today.

Can you name three inventions by women?
Having some difficulty?
Most people do.

For many reasons, female inventors are absent from our imagination. No one doubts that women are ingenious and creative. Yet, few people link women's ideas with invention and the creation of new technologies, products, and services that benefit society at large. Although inventions by women may not be front and centre in our thoughts, women have invented from the beginning of time.

It is more than likely that pre-historic women invented many of the early technologies that helped to advance humanity. These inventions would fall into areas such as food and clothing preparation since women were usually responsible for these tasks. How do we know they invented? Anthropologists tell us that the people who did the work were the ones who came up with creative solutions to make the work less difficult or more productive. Many anthropologists believe that agriculture was invented by women since they were the main food providers in hunter-gatherer times. It makes sense that they would become plant experts, thus the likely inventors of gardening, which later became agriculture.

Even legends and myths from cultures around the world tell the tales of inventive women. The ancient Greeks believed that Athena, the goddess of war and wisdom, invented a large number of technologies including the flute, the earthenware pot, the plow, and the chariot. As well, she was the first to teach mathematics and all women's arts such as cooking and weaving.

Early written documents record the work of several inventive women. The most famous amongst the early inventors is the scientist Hypatia of Alexandria, who was born in A.D. 370. Her specialty was practical technology. She is thought to have contributed to the invention of the plane astrolabe, which measures the position of the sun and stars, as well as the hydrometer, which measures a liquid's specific gravity. Other notable women include the Indian empress Nur Mahal, inventor of the cashmere shawl, and Queen Semiranis of Assyria for her invention of the canal, the bridge, and the causeway.

Throughout history, women faced many barriers that prevented them from advancing their ideas. Up until the 20th century in North America, a woman's place was in the home. Generally, women were not allowed to study, practise sciences, or invent. Despite all this, female inventors persevered. However, information about their inventions usually went unrecorded. Often, the only thing known about a woman's contribution towards the creation of a new technology is anecdotal, sometimes passed down through family stories and letters.

Even after the British Parliament first established the modern-day patent system in 1624 to provide inventors protection under the law, much of the work of female inventors continued to go unrecorded. Patenting an invention was difficult because of attitudes regarding a woman's role in society. American Betsy Metcalf never applied for a patent for her 1798 invention of a new method for braiding straw bonnets. She did not want to be seen as ambitious, which was a highly unladylike characteristic.

As well, property laws that restricted what a woman could own also prevented female inventors from obtaining patents. A single woman could both apply for and do whatever she wanted with a patent. But that changed once she married. Property laws transferred ownership of a woman's property upon marriage to her husband. This included patents, as they can be bought or sold. In some parts of Canada, this situation continued into the early 20th century. As a result, important information about female inventors was lost. Thankfully, laws in Canada and elsewhere changed, giving all women full ownership of their property, and the right to apply for a patent.

Today, a search at the Canadian patent office provides an interesting record of achievement. Although female inventors are still under-represented in the patent records, the number of patents issued yearly to women is growing. Women have a greater opportunity than ever before to develop their ideas, both as professionals and in their private lives. Female inventor organizations around the world have emerged to pro-vide support at all stages of the invention process. This increased role in inventing is putting women at the forefront of developing and creating the processes and products that will define the lifestyle of the future. Soon, we may be able to recall the names of more than three female inventors!

American Elizabeth Howe is an "invisible inventor" whose name does not appear on any patent despite the fact that she helped invent the sewing machine in 1846. Married to Elias Howe, who is credited as the inventor of the sewing machine, she contributed a critical element to its design. It was Elizabeth who came up with the idea to put the eye of the needle in the tip of the needle, which made the machine work. How do we know this? Because Elias told many people what Elizabeth had accomplished.

Did You Know?

Before you find out about Canadian innovation, check out these great inventions from beyond our borders.

Flat Bottom Bag, 1870

Margaret Knight

From a very young age, American Margaret Knight liked to build things. As a young woman, she invented the machinery that folded a piece of paper into a flat bottom bag, an item used today by millions of people around the world. Margaret is credited with over eighty inventions.

Chocolate Chip Cookie, 1933

Ruth Wakefield

American Innkeeper Ruth Wakefield's rush to get chocolate cookies baked quickly led her to chop up chunks of chocolate, which she added to the dough. The chocolate didn't dissolve as she hoped, but stayed in delicious chips. Seventy years later, the cookies still taste great!

Drip Coffee, 1900s

Melitta Bentz

Melitta Bentz of Germany was fed up with drinking grainy coffee made by boiling loose ground coffee in water. So she took a piece of paper from her son's notebook, stuck it in the bottom of a brass can that she had poked full of holes, and invented the coffee filter!

Barbie, 1959

Ruth Handler

Ruth Handler launched an icon when she created the BARBIE doll. At BARBIE's debut in 1959, critics said the doll wouldn't sell. They were proven wrong. In her first eight years, sales reached $500 million. BARBIE, and her companion doll, KEN, are named after Ruth's two children.

Computer Pioneer, 1840s

Ada Byron Lovelace

British Ada Byron Lovelace, the daughter of poet Lord Byron, was a mathematical genius. She was the first to design the punch-card programs that would instruct the analytical engine (proto-computer created in the 1840s by Charles Babbage) in its tasks. Recently, an American military computer programming language was named ADA in her honour.

Computer Compiler, 1952

Rear Admiral Grace Murray Hopper

Computer technology took a huge leap forward when American Rear Admiral Grace Murray Hopper invented the first compiler, which allowed for automatic programming. Previously, computer programmers had to write time-consuming machine instructions for each program. Rear Admiral Hopper also developed COBOL, the first user-friendly business computer software program.

Frequency Hopping, 1940s

Hedy Lamarr

Hedy Lamarr, though originally from Germany, was a famous Hollywood actress. However, few people know she was also an inventor. She invented "frequency hopping", a secret communications tool, during World War II. Although never used by the American military as she had hoped, "frequency hopping" later became the basis of cell phone technology.

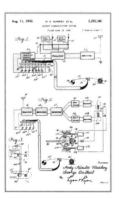

Bra, 1910s and 1920s

Polly Jacob/Ida Cohen Rosenthal

American teenager Polly Jacob turned two silk handker-chiefs and a length of pink ribbon into the first brassiere. The brassiere was a welcome relief from the tight fitting corsets worn by women at the time. Later, another American, Ida Cohen Rosenthal, created a brassiere with shaped cups that came in different sizes. Ida started the Maidenform Brassiere Company in 1923.

Have you ever had a "computer bug?" As the story goes, Rear Admiral Hopper introduced the saying into the English language when she found that a dead moth inside one of her computers was responsible for the computer acting up.

Actress Hedy Lamarr never publicized her invention and few knew of her secret identity as a technologist. In the golden age of Hollywood, image was all-important, and Hedy was sensitive to how the public viewed her. Her patent application was filed under her real name – Hedwig Kiesler. Even fifty years later she refused to be interviewed about her achievement.

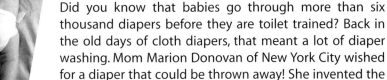

If you went looking for patents by Stephanie Kwolek, you wouldn't find any. The patents are filed under the name S.L. Kwolek, a reminder to us of the time when being female was seen as a disadvantage.

Disposable Diaper, 1951

Marion Donovan

Did you know that babies go through more than six thousand diapers before they are toilet trained? Back in the old days of cloth diapers, that meant a lot of diaper washing. Mom Marion Donovan of New York City wished for a diaper that could be thrown away! She invented the first disposable diaper, which she made out of a plastic shower curtain and absorbent padding.

Canning Process, 1872

Amanda Theodosia Jones

Not only did inventor Amanda Theodosia Jones create a new method for preserving fresh foods in cans, she also started her own company – the U.S. Women's Pure Food Vacuum Preserving Company. The company employed only women!

Kevlar, 1950s

Stephanie Kwolek

Where would the world be without KEVLAR? From bullet-proof vests to tires to canoes, this super strong synthetic fibre revolutionized the way things function and are built. American Stephanie Kwolek invented KEVLAR while working as a chemist at Du Pont Chemicals.

"I certainly feel that the time is not far distant when a knowledge of the principles of diet will be an essential part of one's education."
Fannie Farmer

Scientific Recipes, 1896

Fannie Farmer

For centuries, people used the "pinch," the "handful," or the "heaping cup" method of cooking. In 1896, American Fannie Farmer changed all that when she published the *FANNIE FARMER COOK BOOK*. It was the first cookbook to use scientific measurements, which applied a standard-ized measurement system to cooking. The cookbook is still popular today, more than one hundred years later!

Nonreflecting Glass, 1938

Katherine Blodgett

American physicist Katherine Blodgett was intrigued with a substance which left a coating one molecule thick. No practical use could be thought of until, applying it to glass, she saw that it eliminated all glare. Her discovery was dubbed "invisible glass." Eliminating the reflection on glass helps visibility and improves the efficiency of lenses found in cameras, microscopes, and optical equipment.

Scotchgard, 1950s

Patsy Sherman

This versatile product was the result of an accidental spill! While researching latex for use in jet aircraft, scientists Patsy Sherman and Sam Smith spilled some of their experiment on a tennis shoe. No amount of cleaning could remove it. Over time, that part of the shoe also stayed clean. Intrigued, Patsy and Sam dipped other materials in the latex, and found that they also resisted staining. Today, SCOTCHGARD is applied to all kinds of fabrics to repel liquids and dirt.

Liquid Paper, 1950s

Bette Graham Nesmith

Before computers, typewriters were part of every office. One spelling mistake often meant an entire page had to be re-typed. American secretary Bette Graham Nesmith brought artist's paint from home and used it to correct her mistakes. This labour-saving material was quickly in demand. She named her invention LIQUID PAPER.

The Gardenia, 1770

Jane Colden

Botanist Jane Colden discovered and identified the Gardenia as a species of a new genus never before named. Working in the 1700s, she catalogued more than three hundred regional plant species in New York state, many of which she sketched. Educated and encouraged to excel, she is considered to be one of the first female scientists in the United States.

Between 1863 and 1913, approximately 1,200 inventions were patented by Afro-American inventors. Madame Walker (1867-1919) was a St. Louis washerwoman turned inventor of a method to soften and smooth black women's hair. An astute businesswoman, her invention made her a millionaire, a philanthropist, and an employer of 3,000 people.

"I think anyone who is making progress faces fear. Overcoming fear is all there is to success. You have to face fears and doubts constantly. You keep doing it over and over."
Bette Graham Nesmith

We came to the shores of Newfoundland on the 5th of August. Though the coast was brown, and rugged, and desolate, I hailed its appearance with rapture. Never did anything seem so delicious as the land breeze that came to us, as I thought, bearing health and gladness on its wings.

Catherine Parr Trail, Explorer and Author (1802-1899)
Excerpt from The Backwoods of Canada

Safety First
Alice Dicks

A potential life-and-death situation inspired Grand Falls resident Alice Dicks to invent the HAND GUARD.

In the late 1980s, Alice was working as a blood collection nurse for the Red Cross. Her job involved transferring donor blood into vacutainers (test tubes) for testing. Precisely puncturing the vacutainer's rubber top with a needle was difficult. Alice and her co-workers risked pricking themselves and contaminating themselves with viruses such as HIV.

Then one day, what Alice worried about most happened – she accidentally pricked herself. Alice was unharmed, but the experience unsettled her and she was determined that it would never happen again. She searched the market for a protective guard that could come between her hand and the needle, and found there was nothing commercially available.

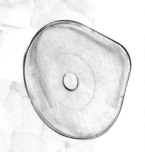

"If you have an idea that you believe in, you should really push and try to have it developed."
Alice Dicks

So Alice took things into her own hands – literally – and created a small hand shield out of the bottom of a plastic bleach bottle. Encouraged by her co-workers' positive reaction to the homemade product and motivated by their suggestions for improvements, she designed a very simple but effective protective device known as the HAND GUARD.

The clear plastic HAND GUARD has one to four circular openings into which the vacutainers are inserted. The healthcare worker holds the vacutainers from below, with the hand shielded by the HAND GUARD. Thanks to Alice's ingenuity and invention, the number of needle-related injuries has decreased greatly, and health care workers feel more protected. The HAND GUARD is sold through Alice's company, Tides Point Holdings.

Safety on the Seas
Mona El-Tahan

Every year, 400-800 icebergs move at a rate of 7km (4 miles) per hour, creeping or flowing stealthily under their own weight down the east coast of Labrador and Newfoundland.

It was a dark and stormy night in Newfoundland. More than eighty workers on board an oil drilling rig on the Grand Banks saw an iceberg on the horizon moving their way. Would the iceberg hit the rig? After one quick telephone call, everyone went to bed, secure in the knowledge that they would be safe.

The call was made to Mona El-Tahan of St. John's, who predicted with 99% certainty that the iceberg would come within one kilometre of the rig, but would not strike it. The next morning the iceberg was exactly where Mona said it would be.

No, Mona is not a psychic. She is an Ice Environment and Information Technology Specialist with a background in engineering. Since the mid-1980s, Mona has designed software and systems to help ships stay on course, avoid icebergs, and manoeuvre in tight waterways such as rivers.

Some of Mona's computer models predict iceberg drift and deterioration. Other software – the first of its kind anywhere – uses statistics and data to provide accurate environmental forecasts. Yet another invention steers ships so precisely that their fuel consumption is cut by up to 10%. Mona's expertise, systems and software are available through her company, Coretec Inc., which she founded in 1988.

Mona is known throughout the worldwide marine industry, both for her inventions, and for the fact that she is a woman working in a male dominated field. Her choice of profession was, as she puts it, "a rather unusual field for a native of Egypt." Because of this, she has received much attention in her birth country. Mona was born in Cairo, and arrived in St. John's in 1975. Mona is dedicated to increasing the numbers of young females entering the engineering and science professions. She founded the Newfoundland Chapter of Women in Science and Engineering.

"It's important to appreciate constructive criticism, and to pass on your knowledge and skills to others, especially young people."
Mona El-Tahan

ideas · ingenuity · passion · creativity · inventiveness · inspiration

Traditional embroidered samplers were more than just an attractive decorative feature in Newfoundland homes. They were also an innovative way for women to transfer information about family history and community events to future generations. Cross-stitch was used to create both words and pictures on the cloth. Often, young girls practised their embroidery skills on samplers, and sometimes the sampler was like a personal diary.

Knit One, Purl Two
Women's War Effort

Who would have thought that knitted socks would create an opportunity for innovation?

During World War I, there was an urgent need for 300,000 pairs of grey socks! Thousands of British Commonwealth troops were fighting overseas in freezing, rain-filled trenches. Morale was slipping. The request for socks propelled the women of Newfoundland into action! Although knitting a pair of socks is simple, the demand for so many created a ground swell of organizations, committees, and social groups in unprecedented numbers.

The interaction of so many skilled women, intent on a common goal, led to innovation in its purest form; the humble sock was made warmer, more comfortable, and better fitting! "Women's work" was now ranked as a highly valued contribution to the war effort. It was said that: "A Newfoundland sock is the best in the world and is prized by every soldier."

A "Motherly" Demonstration
Colleen Dunn-Pickard

A new product provides a valuable learning opportunity for siblings of newborn babies.

In the late-1990s, a first-of-its-kind mother and baby doll set designed to teach about breast-feeding was invented by Colleen Dunn-Pickard of Clarke's Beach. The doll set is in the "Raggedy Ann" style. The mother doll comes dressed in a front-opening shirt, and the baby is attached to the mother in the nursing position using VELCRO. The dolls can be used by pregnant mothers to show their older children what to expect when the baby comes.

The doll set has received an industrial design patent and is sold through Colleen's company, MOTHER NURTURE.

High-Tech Weddings
Jackie Howell

Getting married? Can't find the perfect dress or the right flowers? Look no further. Everything you need is at www.virtuallyhitched.com.

Virtuallyhitched.com was created by Jackie Howell, a young St. John's resident with no previous training in technology. She was among the first in Newfoundland to go on-line offering an innovative and unique service to consumers. Jackie's entry into the "wired world" helped to further a female presence on the Internet in Canada and, in particular, Newfoundland.

The web site helps engaged couples plan their wedding. Once visitors sign up, the system generates directions, budgets, task lists, worksheets, a guest database, an RSVP area, a personalized web page with customized content, and other useful tools. Jackie compares it to a dress rehearsal and says her site helps bridal couples "see" their wedding before it happens. Couples have the opportunity to save time and money, and to avoid costly mistakes.

The web site grew out of a wedding planning company Jackie started when she was only twenty-one years old. She is a role model to other Newfoundlanders who look to her site as an example for taking traditional businesses on-line.

"Believe in yourself and your idea. Surround yourself with experienced people, and then hire people who are smarter than you! Don't be afraid to share your idea, because if you don't, it cannot grow. Follow these guidelines and success will find you."
Jackie Howell

In Praise of Newfoundland
Margaret Duley (1894-1968)

Margaret Duley of St. John's was the first Newfoundland writer to receive international attention and praise for her writing.

From the early 1920s to the 1940s, she wrote novels describing the lives and hardships of Newfoundlanders. She also wrote radio scripts and newspaper articles, and interviewed remarkable women of the time such as Florence Nightingale and singer Jenny Lind. Her passion for Newfoundland was great. Throughout her life, she described and promoted Newfoundland, both within the province and across Canada. As well, she was part of the women's suffrage movement and fought for women's right to vote.

ideas · ingenuity · passion · creativity · inventiveness · inspiration

Prince Edward Island

Lucy Maude Montgomery's book, The Story of Anne of Green Gables, *draws more than 10,000 Japanese travellers to PEI yearly who visit places associated with the book.*

Much of the beauty of the island is due to the vivid colour contrasts – the rich red of the winding roads, the brilliant emerald of the uplands and meadows, and the glowing sapphire of the encircling sea.

Lucy Maude Montgomery, Author (1874-1942)
Excerpt from The Alpine Path: Every Woman's World

"Never be afraid to try. Blaze your own trail."
Catherine Chan

21st Century Science
Catherine Chan

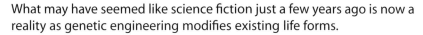

What may have seemed like science fiction just a few years ago is now a reality as genetic engineering modifies existing life forms.

Dr. Catherine Chan, a Professor at the Atlantic Veterinary College of the University of Prince Edward Island, is part of a research team that is using a genetically engineered mouse to closely examine how insulin is made in the body. The mouse was developed by a colleague at Harvard University. The team hopes the mouse will help them find a way to prevent diabetes (which results from lack of insulin), or provide better treatments for the disease.

The mouse has been engineered so that one of its genes is "knocked out." In this case, the "knocked out" gene can no longer translate into a protein. Tests are run on the altered mouse. If the mouse shows high levels of insulin secretion in its body, then the absent protein is important in regulating the insulin levels in normal mice. The tests may help identify which proteins play a role in Type 2 Diabetes Mellitus.

Presently, it is not possible in Canada to obtain a patent for genetically engineered complex life forms. Only lower life forms, such as single-celled organisms, qualify for a patent. Examples include bacteria or yeast cells that have been bioengineered to eliminate pollutants or to do other specific industrial jobs. Because of this restriction, Catherine and her team have applied to the United States government for a patent for the use of the "knock-out" mouse in the study of insulin secretions. The patent application has yet to be approved.

Science Fair Winner
Micheline Briand

A science fair project became a new system to help the environment! Fourteen-year-old Micheline Briand from Charlottetown wanted to find a way to recycle and reuse the 5,000 truckloads of sand, granite and salt dumped on island roads every winter.

The recycling system she invented uses an industrial vacuum cleaner and a series of screens to collect and sort the road debris. To test her theory, Micheline enlisted the assistance of a number of people and organizations, including the National Research Council of Canada, a local environmental consulting company, and the Superintendent of Highway Safety for the Department of Public Works. With their help, Micheline discovered that her experiment not only worked, but the recycled material could also be used to make concrete. In fact, the concrete turned out to be very strong, withstanding more pressure than a commercially produced brand!

"Science is trial and error. I encountered many challenges and roadblocks while I developed and tested my device. There were many technical difficulties but I was lucky to be able to sort them out. I was able to contact and get help from several mentors along the way. Support came from family and friends, but my greatest support came from my parents."
Micheline Briand

Helping Horses Heal
Laurie MacDuffee

It is always heartbreaking when a beloved horse has to be put down because of a broken leg. Leg bone fractures in horses are very difficult to heal on their own and cause terrible suffering for the animals.

Dr. Laurie MacDuffee of the Atlantic Veterinary College of the University of Prince Edward Island hopes her new invention might be a solution. Laurie has developed THE EQUINE INTERLOCKING NAIL, a special medical implant for horses with broken leg bones. Although the device is still in the experimental stage, it may one day help leg bones to mend, thereby saving the lives of injured horses.

From Artist to Healer
Alma Buote MacCormick (1894-1966)

Artistic innovation is not restricted to canvas and paint. Artist Alma Buote MacCormick of Tignish went from working as a successful commercial artist in Prince Edward Island to becoming an innovative designer of artificial limbs for the New York City manufacturer Astrel Laboratories. Although she lived far from home, she never lost her deep love for her Canadian roots. After retiring in 1958, she returned to Prince Edward Island where she founded the Tignish Arts Foundation.

Clean Solutions
Kelly Galloway

When you flush a toilet, down goes the water. Then what? Engineer Kelly Galloway of Charlottetown works hard to ensure that the innovative waste management systems she designs suit the unique needs of her clients as well as the ecological needs of the site.

The work carried out by her company, Engineering Technologies Canada Ltd., is helping to advance our understanding of how to protect the environment from human waste. For example, on a sensitive New Brunswick project, conventional approaches would have required either an effluent discharge pipe to the ocean or large-scale tree cutting to make way for a septic field. Instead, Kelly designed an effluent dispersal system using drip irrigation tubing and wood chips that preserved the natural vegetation and allowed it to help take up the cleared effluent from the treatment system.

"Try to find what interests you, then do it!"
Kelly Galloway

Giving it a Name
Constance Ida MacFarlane (1904-1999)

Seaweed is more than just a wrap around a sushi roll. It comes in many forms with intriguing names like Irish moss, dulse, rockweed, and kelp.

Today, thanks to Marine Biologist Dr. Constance Ida MacFarlane, all the different varieties of seaweed in the rich waters of the Atlantic are known. In 1929, Constance conducted the first-ever extensive survey of the seaweeds and marine algae of the Maritime provinces. The survey had a great impact on seaweed harvesting practises, contributing to the development of harvesting techniques, and conservation programs. In 1949, Constance was appointed head of the Seaweeds Division of the Nova Scotia Research Foundation in Halifax. She received numerous prestigious national awards for her work, including the Canadian Centennial Medal. The medal commemorated the one-hundredth anniversary of the Confederation of Canada.

Inventing for a Changing World
Irene Novaczek

One day, tasty candy made from sea licorice and thorn grass seaweed may be on your shopping list. These are just two of the unique food products invented by Marine Botanist and Environmentalist Dr. Irene Novaczek of Breadalbane.

Although Irene has invented many things, she says the most innovative thing she has done is to re-invent herself to suit a changing world with changing needs. She has not remained tied to marine botany, but has applied her knowledge of "how to learn" and "how to discover things" to a wide range of topics. Starting with seaweed ecology, she moved into microbiology, shellfish toxicology, and small business and product development.

Irene is committed to enabling the poorest in society to develop self-sustaining small businesses based on local resources. She believes this work is truly "inventive" since there is usually little money to work with. As well, the equipment, processes, and recipes must change often to suit difficult circumstances.

"Shake off the ties that bind your mind. Be an explorer. Get out into the world and take risks."
Irene Novaczek

Safe Art, Anyone?
Debra Percival

Did you know that making art can be hazardous to your health? The fumes from many materials used to make sculptures, photographs, paintings, and prints, as well as the solvents needed for cleaning up, can be toxic.

Concerned about potential health hazards, Charlottetown printmaker Debra Percival developed new printmaking methods and non-toxic materials that allow printmaking to be carried out safely. Debra's non-toxic approach is not only unique, it also allows for greater creativity and expression since artists no longer feel restricted by the fear of toxicity. Through the Internet, she connects with artists from around the world, sharing information about her new methods and materials.

"Nothing ever works the first time. Just be patient."
Debra Percival

BABY SAFE for Safe Babies
Beverly Brodie

In 1994, Dr. Beverly Brodie of Charlottetown received Trademark #TMA421768 for BABY SAFE, a device which keeps a sleeping baby securely positioned on his or her side. It consists of two rice-filled weights joined by a pad.

21

New Brunswick

People went ashore and brought on board some pea vines with blossoms on them, also some gooseberries, spruce and grass, all of which grew wild. They say this is to be our city. Our land is five and twenty miles up the river.

Sara Frost, Settler
Diary excerpt describing her 1783 arrival at Fort Howe

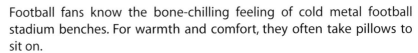

Measures Heat
Nancy Mathis

Football fans know the bone-chilling feeling of cold metal football stadium benches. For warmth and comfort, they often take pillows to sit on.

Believe it or not, the cloth pillow and the metal bench are the same temperature. The metal bench feels colder because it has a higher heat transfer ability than cloth. This means that the metal bench lets heat from the body leave faster. Welcome to the amazing world of thermal conductivity!

In 1995, Fredericton Chemical Engineer Dr. Nancy Mathis launched her invention – the TC PROBE, an electrical device that measures thermal conductivity in materials. The device tests foams, insulation, pastes, adhesives, polymers, ceramics, glass, silicon, and natural fibers. It works by heating a sample of the material being tested. The temperature change in the sample is measured, and from this the thermal properties of the material become known. The test is completed in a matter of seconds.

Knowing about thermal conductivity in different materials is very important for industries that build items like computers and appliances. The information helps companies save money and create products that are more energy efficient. IBM (computers), ExxonMobil (petroleum), and Dow Corning (composite materials) are just a few of the companies that use the TC PROBE as part of the manufacturing process.

"Innovation is having and acting on a good idea. I am lucky to have a stimulating environment and diverse exposure which helps me generate ideas."
Nancy Mathis

22

Big Fish
Debbie Martin-Robichaud

Did you ever hear a fisherman talk about "the big one that got away?" Well, that fish is about to get even bigger!

Marine Biologist Debbie Martin-Robichaud works for the Government of Canada's Department of Fisheries and Oceans. Debbie specializes in growing fish (mostly halibut and haddock) larger and at a faster pace. Using molecular selective breeding techniques, she hopes to improve production on fish farms. Since females grow faster and bigger than males in many fish species, Debbie is developing breeding methods which produce only female fish.

According to the Department of Fisheries and Oceans, Canadian fisheries are a billion-dollar industry. An increasing number of fish are now being grown on fish farms (aquaculture). Debbie's breeding methods will hopefully create a competitive edge for Canadian fish farmers over fish farmers worldwide. Fish and chips, anyone?

"Try to make a job out of something that you really enjoy doing, because you could be doing that same thing for the rest of your life."
Debbie Martin-Robichaud

Trucking Software
Carole Daley

Inventor Carole Daley from Miramichi is helping to bring high-tech innovations to the old-fashioned world of trucking.

Before her invention of the FUEL FASTAX software in 1998, trucking firms and independent carriers had to file complicated fuel tax reports for the International Fuel Tax Agreement (IFTA). FUEL FASTAX is an on-line application (efueltax.com) that saves time and money by streamlining these reports. Truckers enter trip details on-line, and the software automatically calculates and prints IFTA forms for convenient filing.

Today, Carole and her staff at ALT Group Inc. are developing a wireless application for hand-held computers and mobile phones. The project, which is partly funded by the National Research Council of Canada, will also involve an Internet site called www.etruckingsolutions.com. It will help truckers stay in touch with their families, while allowing them to research fuel prices and road conditions on their route.

"Do your research, identify a niche that you can add to, build what the market wants, and build the best."
Carole Daley

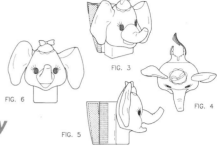

FIG. 3

FIG. 6

FIG. 4

FIG. 5

Keeps Baby Happy
Barbara Michaud

New Brunswick inventor Barbara Michaud says the process of inventing is like raising a child. Both require complete dedication, hard work, a willingness to learn, and a lot of perseverance.

Barbara came up with the idea for her invention in 1994 after she became tired of always having to search for her baby's pacifier in and around the crib. To solve the problem, she created an animal-shaped pacifier holder. The holder attaches to the side of the crib, and the pacifier is held in the animal's mouth. The easy-to-use device positions the pacifier within reach of the baby.

Since then, Barbara has had to learn about patents, manufacturing, molds, and other aspects of product development in order to turn a good idea into a commercial success. In 1998, after four years of hard work, she developed a prototype for the pacifier holder. Manufacturing is expected to begin soon, which goes to show that time and persistence can turn struggle into reward. Any mother knows that!

"You have to have a vision, and be able to visualize your product in stores. Once you start working on your invention, it becomes part of your life."
Barbara Michaud

A Must See
Muriel Lutes Sikorski (1909-1984)

Muriel Lutes Sikorski saw the economic potential in an unusual Moncton area geographic phenomena – a hill that appeared as if it was magnetic. She gave it the name it is known by today – Magnetic Hill. Though Magnetic Hill is nothing more than a wonderful, bizarre optical illusion, it attracts thousands of tourists annually who want to see the illusion of their cars coasting backwards up the hill.

Muriel didn't stop there. In 1933, with $35.00, she opened the Magnetic Hill Gift Shop. In 1973, it was the largest gift shop in Atlantic Canada.

Prevents Accidents
Lise Devost Reckler

For those who live in big cities, the prospect of streets without street-lamps may seem foreign. But, in Lise Devost Reckler's hometown of St. Anne, few roadways are lit. Poor visibility at night led to many people being injured, or even killed by motorists. Sadly, Lise's uncle was a fatality.

Following the tragic death of her uncle, Lise decided to take action. In 1994, she invented the PROTEXION PLUS HARNESS for joggers and pedestrians. The harness consists of highly reflective straps that cross in an X on the chest and back of the wearer. The harness is visible to motorists up to one mile away.

Lise has made many personal sacrifices to develop and launch her invention. She has invested her own savings, and a tremendous amount of time and energy. The day she received her patent, she was so over-whelmed by emotion that she cried. Though she has manufactured several thousand harnesses and has secured patents in Canada and the United States, she has yet to achieve widespread distribution. Lise says it will take much more time, money and determination on her part before people can easily purchase her product in their local stores.

"Never give up. Follow your dreams."
Lise Devost Reckler

Despite her struggles, Lise continues to passionately believe that her invention will help keep joggers and pedestrians safe on the streets. She now sells the PROTEXION PLUS HARNESS over the Internet, and through catalogue sales in the United States. She hopes one day soon, the harness will become a standard safety accessory. Lise credits her daughter as her greatest supporter during her journey as an inventor.

Radio and Television Legend
Mary Grannan (1900-1975)

Fredericton native Mary Grannan invented the radio and television programs "Just Mary" and "Maggie Muggins," which were listened to and seen on CBC from 1939 to 1962. The programs were so popular that the names of the programs became household words in Canada.

Nova Scotia

While waiting to be processed as new arrivals at Pier 21, we were greeted by the friendliest of people who offered us food and clothing for our children. We thought if all Canadians were as kind and helpful as those in Halifax, then our decision to come to Canada was a good one.

Vera Ouroumoff, New Canadian
Interview excerpt describing her 1951 arrival in Canada

Absorbs Heat
Mary Anne White

Have you ever warmed your hands around a cup of tea or a mug of hot chocolate? If so, consider yourself a recycler of heat. The heat that was originally generated by a stove, electric kettle, or microwave to boil the drink was used to heat another object – YOU!

Dr. Mary Anne White of Halifax knows a lot about heat and the thermal properties of materials. Since the early-1990s, she has worked on the development of a new class of heat-absorbing chemicals that recycle leftover heat from industrial processes. Compared to other chemicals used for this purpose, Mary Anne's heat-absorbing chemicals hold more heat, and for a longer period of time. They also stay in a solid form, and don't melt or float away when they gain or lose heat – a problem faced by other similar chemicals. In the future, the heat-absorbing chemicals, and the process developed for their use, will help companies and consumers waste less energy. The chemicals are now being tested in a solar powered home in the Halifax area.

Mary Anne is the Killam Research Professor in Materials Science at Dalhousie University. She believes that graduating in the 1970s from MacMaster University in Ontario was the perfect time to enter her field. An energy crisis had turned North America's attention to conservation. At that same time, women were being welcomed into the scientific community more so than a decade earlier. Mary Anne has some advice for young scientists. She believes that achieving success is a long-term proposition and, in spite of setbacks, it is important to never give up.

"Don't give up! Have faith in yourself!"
Mary Anne White

Behind the Scenes Dynamo
Mabel Bell (1857-1923)

Behind the scenes, an unknown dynamo helped Canada soar in the skies. Mabel Bell, wife of renowned inventor Alexander Graham Bell, was herself an innovative force. Besides being an avid supporter of the inventive work of her husband, she made a significant contribution to Canadian aviation history.

Mabel, deaf since the age of five, was a visionary in her own right. In 1907, her passionate enthusiasm for the new science of flight led her to invest her $35,000 inheritance toward founding and supporting the Aerial Experiment Association. She sought out pioneering aviation engineers, manufacturers, and pilots, and brought them together to share ideas and to help her husband with his aviation inventions.

The Aerial Experiment Association succeeded in building four historically important planes: the Red Wing, the White Wing, the June Bug, and the Silver Dart. All of these were made and flown in Canada. The AEA also initiated new building techniques that were used by later aviators, including the use of linseed oil to seal the fabric on wings.

Mabel is quoted as saying: "The Aerial Experiment Association was a great, marvelous success, yet very few know this; fewer still know the magnitude of that success. It accomplished what it set out to do, which was to evolve a practical type of flying machine."

Taking off from the ice-covered waters of Baddeck Bay, Nova Scotia, the Silver Dart made the first powered flight in Canada on February 23, 1909.

Art School Founder
Anna Leonowens (1834-1915)

Anna Leonowens had little idea while working in the Court of Siam (present day Thailand) as governess to the King's sixty-four children that her experience would inspire the stage musical *The King and I*, and the film *Anna and the King*.

After leaving Siam, Anna moved to Canada and lived in Halifax from 1876-1897. During her time in Nova Scotia, she pioneered many social programs and cultural institutions. One such achievement was the establishment of the Victoria School of Art, now known as the Nova Scotia College of Art and Design. The school was founded to honour Queen Victoria's Golden Jubilee. Anna died in Montreal in 1915.

27

Pedal to the Metal!

Highland Thunder Electric Racing

Ingenuity and teamwork paid off on the electric formula race car track for the only all-female team in the world.

In 1998, eight dynamic and inventive Port Hawkesbury high school students took a retired formula race car, and rebuilt it into an award winning electric formula race car. Known as Highland Thunder Electric Racing, team members Elisa Conner, Cara Dawson, Janine Goyetche, Cheryl Kawaja, Arnie MacDonald, Nicole MacDonald, Erin MacIntyre and Natalie MacKeigan won the U.S. Championships at the APS Electric Race. The race was held in Arizona and sponsored by the Arizona Public Service Company.

Highland Thunder Electric Racing was one of only two high school teams to enter the competition, and the only high school team to race an electric formula race car. One of the team's members also set a record for drag racing in her division.

To build the car, the team applied their skills in welding, machining, mechanics, and electronics. As well, in order to travel to Arizona they raised an impressive $20,000 from six thousand supportive community members, and corporate sponsors.

The team's ingenuity led to some last-minute design improvements, such as a hair dryer cooling fan and the use of a plastic TUPPERWARE lid to protect the electronics. These two additions improved the performance of the vehicle and contributed to its sweeping victory.

The team has used the vehicle to promote women in science, and to increase awareness of electric vehicles and their benefit to the environment. Presently, the car is in storage at Janine Goyetche's home in Port Hawkesbury. The team hopes that one day the car might find a permanent home in the local museum.

"A lot of people told us it couldn't be done, but we worked together and proved them wrong. The fact that we had built a car worthy of competition was a bigger accomplishment than winning the race."
Janine Goyetche

A Clean Sweep
Anna Sutherland Bissell

Canadian ingenuity created a North American household icon! For more than a hundred years, people across the continent have reached for the BISSELL CARPET SWEEPER to clean the floors of their homes. The cleaning machine was co-invented by Anna Sutherland Bissell, who was born in Pictou County. In the mid-1800s, Anna often became frustrated with cleaning the sawdust that was embedded in the carpet of her small crockery shop in Grand Rapids, Michigan. Tiny, stubborn particles clung to the carpet, and sweeping them up was time-consuming and frustrating.

The problem was solved when Anna, with her husband Melville, designed and built a carpet sweeper machine. The machine was a success, and people soon began asking where they could purchase a sweeper for themselves. The BISSELL CARPET SWEEPER was patented in 1876. In 1883, the first manufacturing plant was built in Grand Rapids, Michigan. Following Melville Bissell's death in 1889, Anna Bissell stepped in and confidently took control of the company, becoming America's first female corporate CEO. Since 1907, the BISSELL CARPET SWEEPER has been manufactured in Niagara Falls, Ontario.

Toxin Test
Joanne Fraser Jellett

Shellfish toxins are extremely dangerous to humans. In fact, eating just one poisoned clam or mussel can result in death from paralytic shellfish poisoning (PSP). Government testers and food processors often check for shellfish toxins by injecting mice with samples taken from the shellfish. This kind of testing takes time, and kills the mice who either die from the toxin or from the shock of being injected.

Dr. Joanne Fraser Jellett of Chester Basin found an alternative testing method that did not involve the use of mice. Since 1995, Joanne has been involved in the commercialization of a user-friendly diagnostic kit for paralytic shellfish poison, and the development of similar kits for other types of biotoxins. The diagnostic kit is a chemical-based tool that is fast and inexpensive. Now, government testers and food processors can get the information they need quickly.

Joanne says early exposure to science led her to pursue scientific studies at the University of Calgary, the Bedford Institute of Oceanography, and the University of Glasgow. For more than twenty years, she has worked as a Microbiologist in both the medical and marine fields. Joanne is President and CEO of her own company, Jellett Biotek Ltd.

"If you think you have something the world wants or needs to buy, then you have the opportunity to create a business out of it."
Joanne Fraser Jellett

ideas • ingenuity • passion • creativity • inventiveness • inspiration

Quebec

You would think you had just come upon the antiquated heart of some sleepy small town. All is placid and serene. The hundred-year old trees that flood this corner of Montreal with shade link their boughs and form a peaceful avenue that gives shelter to houses with quiet facades.

Gabrielle Roy, Author (1909-1980)
Letter excerpt

Delivery Room CALM
Emily Hamilton

An Associate Professor of Obstetrics and Gynecology at McGill University, Dr. Emily Hamilton has helped bring CALM to hospital delivery rooms across North America.

Emily was disturbed by the number of babies unnecessarily delivered by Caesarean operation in North America. Her concerns led her to design CALM (Computer Assisted Labour Monitoring System), a computer system which monitors the progress of mother and baby during childbirth.

During labour, the user-friendly computer system collects data such as information about the mother's contractions and the baby's heart rate. CALM displays and interprets the data to give the physician a precise assessment of how the labour is advancing by comparing the mother to a large reference population of similar women who delivered normally. The invention was first available to hospitals in Canada and the U.S. in 1998.

The Right Fit
Annie Maud McIntyre

Have you ever worn a sock that was way too big? If you have, you know how awkward it can feel.

Knitter Annie Maud McIntyre invented a tool called MEASURE FOR FOOTWEAR to help knitters make socks for differently-sized and-shaped feet. The device consisted of a measuring tape with markings that showed the precise dimensions of the rib, leg, heel, and toe for socks in various sizes. In 1918, she received Canadian Patent #185952.

Medical Titan
Maude Abbott (1869-1940)

Pathologist Dr. Maude Abbott is a titan of Canadian medical history. Among her many achievements, Maude is known around the world for inventing the first international classification system for congenital heart disease. Through her careful study of congenital heart defects (heart problems that people are born with), Maude contributed to the advancement of cardiac surgery. Maude's intensive medical research also dramatically improved the life expectancy of infants with heart disorders.

Maude's career was launched in 1908, when one of her research papers was published in Sir William Osler's book, *Modern Medicine*. The ground-breaking paper was based on the research findings of over four hundred congenital heart disease cases. Osler's book brought her international recognition. Almost thirty years later, she capped her career with her book, the *Atlas of Congenital Cardiac Disease,* which was published in 1936. During her lifetime, Maude wrote over one hundred and forty papers and books.

Maude was born in 1869 and raised in the town of St. Andrews East. Bright, hard-working, and dedicated, she earned a scholarship to attend Royal Victoria College for women. At the time, the college was affiliated with Montreal's McGill University. Although Maude could study many subjects, she was not allowed to study medicine as only men were permitted into McGill University's medical program. Following graduation in 1890, Maude entered Bishop's Medical College in Montreal. She was finally able to pursue her passion for medicine, eventually graduating in 1894. During her four years at the school, she was the only woman in her classes.

Almost two decades later, Maude was given what she had been denied. In 1910, McGill University awarded her an honourary medical degree, even though women were still refused entry into its medical program. She was also given a teaching position, which she held for many years. Despite her fame and achievements, the university never promoted her beyond Assistant Professor. Maude never married. She died from a stroke at the age of seventy-one. In 1994, Maude was posthumously inducted into the Canadian Medical Hall of Fame.

"I was consumed by an intense thirst for the school work, and hurled myself into it with tremendous zest, with the result that I was fortunate as to win the scholarship into McGill from the school."
Maude Abbott

What's so bad about contaminated soil? Lots. Contaminated soil can kill, or change the plants growing in it. Also, when it rains, the contamination is carried to the underground water table where the earth's water is stored.

Super Detective
Sabrina Perri

It took a curious mind to find a way to detect the unseen.

In 1992, Sabrina Perri of Montreal was looking for an idea for a science fair project. The grade nine high school student was already a seasoned science fair participant, winning numerous awards for her inventions. She came up with the idea to develop a device that could better expose pollution in water and soil, as well as measure toxicity levels. In 1995, after three years of research and development, Sabrina introduced the MICROBIOLUMISCAN at the Montreal Regional Science Fair. The hand-held electronic device detects biopollutants such as E. coli, and other pollutants such as aluminum and copper. The instrument uses a 21st century "magic ingredient" – bacteria that light up when they come into contact with pollutants. The bacteria, an invention by Dr. Michael DuBow and Dr. Angelina Guzzo of McGill University, were genetically engineered to be bioluminescent. The amount of light the bacteria emit reflects the extent of the contamination in the substance being monitored.

Sabrina's invention won her fourteen major awards, including first place at the 1996 Tucson International Science and Engineering Fair. It gave her the opportunity to meet Queen Elizabeth and Canadian Astronaut Roberta Bondar, and to travel to the International Science Fair in Kuwait.

A Helping Hand
Madeleine Johnson

Frustration is often a stepping stone to invention. This was the case for Madeleine Johnson of St. Lambert. She found collecting raked leaves into a plastic garbage bag to be a huge and frustrating chore. To make the task easier, she invented the HOLD-A-BAG. The device consists of a curved metal wire that keeps the top of the bag open while leaves are being placed inside. It also has prongs that fasten the bag to the ground. As she says: "The idea was a simple one born out of necessity." In 1985, she received Canadian Patent #1198720.

Astronaut Mentor
Julie Payette

In June of 1999, Julie Payette fulfilled a childhood dream when she ventured into space as a crew member aboard the Space Shuttle Discovery. Her skill and innovative work helped make the mission a success, and made Julie a role model for all space-loving Canadian females.

The shuttle carried supplies and equipment to the International Space Station for inhabitants who would arrive a year and a half later. As well, the station was in bad condition and required numerous repairs. Drawing on her background in electrical engineering, Julie operated the Canadarm (which is used to deploy and retrieve satellites from the Space Shuttle), helped repair the electrical system, coordinated and supervised the space walk, tended to the photography and recording equipment, and served on the flight deck during the return to Earth. On the second last day before returning, she ejected the Starshine educational satellite into space. Julie looks forward to continuing her work as an astronaut, and participating in future space missions. She says: "I have the best job on Earth!"

Mother and Daughter Team
Sarah and Alexandra Levy

Sarah and Alexandra Levy are an innovative mother and daughter team from Montreal who are making dining easier and more pleasant for people with special needs. They have designed insulated, ergonomic dishes suitable for use by arthritis sufferers, paraplegic persons, and those experiencing coordination difficulties. The dishes are sold through Ergogrip Inc., the company they founded in 1998. Their latest product is the SARALEX plate and cover.

Ergonomically designed dishes vastly improve the quality of life for people with disabilities. The dishes make it possible for users to consume more food, to eat with dignity, and with far greater autonomy than with conventional dishes.

Thinking about becoming an astronaut? The Canadian Space Agency says:

1) Earn at least one advanced degree in science or engineering.

2) Become proficient in more than one discipline.

3) Become a good public speaker.

4) Demonstrate concern for others by taking part in community activities.

5) Maintain your physical fitness.

6) Acquire a background of knowledge in aerospace topics.

7) Obtain experience as a pilot, parachute jumper, and scuba diver.

8) Work for an aerospace company during school breaks in order to get hands-on experience.

33

NO SEW HEM and THE HEELER
Joan Birchwood

For Joan Birchwood, inventing runs in the family. Her father invented the continuous zipper. Her cousin, Anatol Josepho, is the famous American inventor of the PHOTOMATON, sometimes referred to as the "photo booth." Previous to that, Josepho patented a mixing device which permitted hot and cold water to pass through a single faucet, rather than separate ones. This invention is in use worldwide.

In the mid-1960s, Joan was a Montreal mother of two little girls. She was frequently shortening or lengthening her daughters' dresses. To save time and effort, she invented the NO SEW HEM, a dress modification that instantly adjusted the hem up or down without sewing. The invention was patented in four countries.

Joan's fifth and most successful invention to date is THE HEELER for female drivers. Joan had a strong passion for shoes; consequently, she was continuously frustrated with ruining them while driving. To solve the problem, Joan designed an adjustable nylon pouch to fit over the heels and backs of shoes and boots. This patented covering, anchored with an ankle strap, prevents dirt and scuff marks from damaging footwear that rubs against the car floor. THE HEELER has sold in shoe shops and department stores across North America.

"Lucky me. Ideas keep coming – sometimes overnight! The tricky part is determining whether to pursue an idea or abandon it. Abandoning the idea is difficult only for the moment. Pursuing it is a long and arduous path. But when the end justifies the means, the rewards are amazing!"
Joan Birchwood

First Patent in Quebec!
Irene (Felicite) Marais

In 1866, Irene (Felicite) Marais became the first woman in Quebec to receive a Canadian Patent and Trademark for her invention of a cleaning product called ENGLISH CLEANSING FLUID.

Mother of Invention
Giovanna Giancaspro

Meet another Canadian "Mother of Invention." Giovanna Giancaspro of Montreal was inspired by a problem faced by numerous Canadian parents teaching their children to skate.

Like many moms and dads, Giovanna's back hurt as she leaned over her tiny daughter, holding onto her hands to provide balance. Frustrated, Giovanna thought that there had to be a better way. Overnight, she invented the SKI N SKATE harness. Within two days, Giovanna's daughter was gliding on the ice unassisted.

The SKI N SKATE harness helps children learn to balance on ice. It has straps for parents to hold onto from above and loops for children to grasp onto for security. The harness can also be used to teach children how to in-line skate and ski.

Understanding the Brain
Brenda Milner

Dr. Brenda Milner of Montreal is considered to be one of the pioneers of neuro-psychology. Her detailed long-term studies of the brain have added substantially to the scientific understanding of the structure of the brain, especially those areas that control learning, memory, and speech functions.

She carried out her work at McGill University and the Montreal Neurological Institute, starting in the early 1950s. Today, she continues her association with these two schools as a distinguished lecturer in brain research. In 1984, Brenda was named Officer of the Order of Canada and, in 1985, Officier de l'Ordre nationale du Québec. In 1997, she was inducted into the Canadian Medical Hall of Fame.

"Never give up, never stop. Keep pushing until you get there. My biggest fear was talking to the 'big guys', but they're just people too. Also have fun."
Giovanna Giancaspro

Making Patents Possible for Women!
Marie Lacoste Gérin-Lajoie (1867-1945)

Marie Lacoste Gérin-Lajoie dedicated her life to improving the status of Quebec women. A self-taught legal expert, she worked towards reforming the Quebec Civil Code which attributed married women the inferior legal status of a minor, effectively preventing them from controlling their own assets. In 1907, she co-founded the Fédération nationale Saint-Jean-Baptiste, an organization of Francophone women committed to the promotion of civil and political rights for women.

Ontario

The land still draws me more than any other lands. I have lived in Africa and in England, but splendid as they both can be, they do not have the same power to move me in the same way as, for example, that part of southern Ontario where I spent four months last summer in a cedar cabin beside a river.

Margaret Laurence, Author (1928-1987)
Letter excerpt

Aeroplane Builder
Elsie MacGill (1905-1980)

"I was always a sort of Miss Fix-it around the house. I was interested in radio work so I started out planning to be a radio engineer."
Elsie MacGill

In a war heroes comic book, Elsie MacGill was affectionately called "The Queen of the Hurricanes" in honour of her important work during World War II.

Elsie was born in 1905 in Vancouver, but later moved to Ontario to attend the University of Toronto. In 1927, she became the first woman in Canada to obtain an applied science degree in Electrical Engineering. Two years later, she became the first woman in North America to graduate with a master's degree in Aeronautical Engineering, which she received from the University of Michigan. She accomplished this in spite of becoming ill with polio in her last year of study. Throughout the rest of her life, she used crutches to move about.

In the late 1930s, Elsie accepted the position of Chief Aeronautical Engineer in the aircraft division of the Canadian Car and Foundry Company in Fort William, Ontario. It was here that she designed the Maple Leaf Trainer II, which was the first aircraft to be designed by a woman. The aircraft's innovative features gave student pilots greater visibility and stability during take-offs and landings.

When the company won a contract to produce Hurricane Hawker fighter planes for the British government, Elsie, as Chief Engineer, was put in charge of the operation. She re-designed components of the plane, oversaw the design and manufacture of the tools needed for production, and supervised a staff of more than four thousand people. She also developed a winterized version of the plane, equipped with de-icers and skis to make it more suitable for use in northern climates. The Hurricane was used by the British Royal Air Force (RAF) during World War II, where it was instrumental in the Battle of Britain.

In 1943, Elsie opened her own office in Toronto where she worked as an electrical engineering consultant. Over the next several decades, she provided services to both private companies and the government, establishing herself as a leading figure in the aeronautics industry.

The Battle of Britain was the first major battle fought entirely in the air. The German Luftwaffe and the British Royal Air Force fought in the skies over Britain from June to October, 1940. The Hurricane destroyed more German airplanes than the entire Royal Air Force combined, thereby preventing Germany's takeover of England.

"Queen of the Hurricanes," National Archives of Canada

Looking at the Atmosphere
Stella Melo

Today, the impact of human activities on the environment is a great concern. Important questions such as ozone depletion, climate change, and tropospheric pollution can only be answered based on global and long term monitoring of the atmospheric conditions. As a Doctor in Atmospheric Science, Stella Melo is developing and operating optical equipment that measure the concentration of atmospheric species related to the ozone chemistry. This work has taken her to challenging environments like the Canadian Arctic. The research is being carried out in the Department of Physics at the University of Toronto.

"Women are naturally creative and inventive. It is not easy to run a family and work full time, but it is possible and can be enjoyable. Every woman deserves the high of trying!"
Stella Melo

Mother of Invention
Marsha Forchuk Skrypuch

Throughout history, many inventions have been developed by new mothers looking for better products to help them in their new role. In the late 1980s, nursing mom Marsha Forchuk Skrypuch of Brantford couldn't find the right kind of pad to stop breast milk from leaking through her clothes. All available products were unsuitable as they were either expensive, uncomfortable or, as in the case of disposable pads, bad for the environment. Fuelled by her own need and concern for the environment, Marsha invented NURSING MOTHER BREAST PADS. Though the pads look deceptively simple, lots of "design engineering" went into their construction to make them comfortable and easy to use. The pads are still hot sellers thirteen years later!

CPR is a life-saving procedure that can re-start hearts that have stopped because of heart attacks and other reasons such as drowning.

A New Life Saving Tool
Dianne Croteau

Learning how to save lives was made easier when ACTAR 911, a light-weight and affordable mannequin designed to teach people CPR (cardiopulmonary resuscitation), hit the market. Toronto Industrial Designer Dianne Croteau and her partner, Richard Brault, created ACTAR 911 in 1985. Its innovative design makes it portable (ten fit in a duffel bag) and suitable for wet conditions such as lifeguard training.

First Canadian Patent Issued to a Woman
Ruth Adams

In 1855, Ruth Adams became the first woman in Canada to receive a patent for a new technological marvel – the REVERSE COOKING STOVE. At the time, Ruth lived in Toronto in Upper Canada, present day Ontario. Confederation was still twelve years away, so the Letters Patent for her invention was issued to her by the British Government. Her design for the REVERSE COOKING STOVE was unique, and her patent application stated "...that she hath invented a reverse cooking stove, not known in this province by others before her invention."

Why was the cooking stove called "reverse"? It is unclear, although we do know that the stove was designed to have multiple functions. It provided a warming oven, a cook stove and top, and also served as a furnace to warm the kitchen. The stove consisted of individual units that could be used separately or together, making the stove energy efficient since only those parts that were being used needed fuel.

Remembering Family
Plum Johnson

Plum Johnson from Toronto turned a family tradition into a new product for the holiday season. Every year at Christmas, when Plum's children were young, she brought long-distance relatives closer to home by decorating her Christmas tree with their pictures. The photos were glued onto wooden curtain rings, which she had painted.

As the size of the extended family expanded in number, Plum looked for a commercial product that could replace the handmade ornament, thereby saving her time. Not able to find one, in 1995 Plum invented the PICTURE BALL, a clear 3-dimensional ornament designed to hold two photographs back to back.

In one year, Plum took her invention from the design phase to major mass markets. She consulted with engineers, made prototypes, found a factory to manufacturer the PICTURE BALL, designed the box, trade-marked the name, patented the design, and more. She had no idea how difficult it would be, but she persevered. Today her invention is distributed by the Christmas ornament company, Alderbrook Industries, which has licensed the worldwide rights.

"I don't believe people get ideas. I believe ideas get people."
Plum Johnson

39

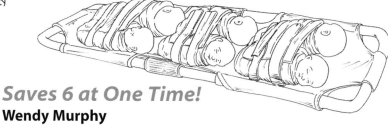

Saves 6 at One Time!
Wendy Murphy

A terrible tragedy inspired a lifesaving invention. In 1985, Mexico was struck by a devastating earthquake. While watching a television news report on the disaster, Wendy Murphy of Toronto saw rescue workers carrying a stretcher which held one tiny infant covered by a small rag. She thought there had to be a way to transport children more efficiently, and in a manner that would keep them warm and secure. Her answer was the WEEVAC 6 emergency evacuation stretcher.

Wendy, a research technician at the Hospital for Sick Children, designed and developed the infant stretcher in 1989. It is the only stretcher in the world that can carry six newborn babies at one time.

Fire resistant material and a lightweight aluminum frame make the WEEVAC 6 strong, durable, and highly reliable in an emergency situation. The narrow stretcher can be easily maneuvered through stairwells. The pockets are made from Mylar laminated vinyl fabric, which helps in retaining the infants' body heat. Each pocket has room for two newborns (from premature to full term). The babies are held securely in place with VELCRO straps.

Wendy won numerous awards for her invention. In 1992, she received the Manning Innovation Award, and the Sir Joseph Flavelle Award for Technical Innovation. She also received the National Research Council of Canada 75th Anniversary Award for outstanding innovativeness in medical device technology.

A New Material
Emillie Caston

On April 1, 1887, Emillie Caston received Canadian Patent #26361 for a manufacturing process that turned thistledown into a material suitable for export to markets outside Canada.

"You can't look at anything as a failing. Everything is a learning experience. If you keep trying and keep enjoying what you do, you can't fail."
Wendy Murphy

The Manning Innovation Award was founded in 1982 to recognize and encourage innovation in Canada.

Mining Breakthroughs
Ann Gallie

In Sudbury, Environmental Earth Scientist Dr. Ann Gallie and her research partner, Benoit Rivard, are designing a 21st century technology for the mining industry.

Although a prototype has yet to be built, the HYPERSPECTRAL REFLECTANCE CORE LOGGER will use artificial light (some of which is invisible to the human eye) to analyse the composition of exposed rock. The device will operate underground where it will readily analyse the rock core samples as they are extracted from the rock by miners. The light that is shone on the rock core sample will reflect different colours based on the kinds of minerals that are present in the rock. This data will then be sent to the on-site geologist and mine manager, who will use the information to determine where it is best to mine. The technology could one day reduce the need to bring rock core samples to the earth's surface for analysis. The machine will thereby save time, human and mechanical effort, and money.

"A researcher always builds on existing research."
Ann Gallie

Cosy Paws
Marianne Bertrand

Search and rescue dogs looking for survivors in the World Trade Centre tragedy of September 11, 2001 needed help. The debris was hot and jagged. The New York City Police Department called Marianne Bertrand, President of Muttluks Inc. They asked for her product – MUTTLUKS leather-soled protective booties for dogs – to equip their search and rescue canine unit. Marianne donated over eight hundred sets – enough to cover the paws of more than three hundred dogs, including the thirty-dog NYPD unit, that were sniffing through the debris.

"Stick with it!"
Marianne Bertrand

Marianne came up with the concept for MUTTLUKS in 1994, when she couldn't find suitable boots for her own dogs. She launched her company, Muttluks Inc., with the FLEECE LINED MUTTLUKS boot. Marianne knew her product was a hit when the first one hundred-thirty sets sold out in less than a week to Toronto pet stores. She has since created an all-weather version. MUTTLUKS are named after the Inuit sealskin boots "Mukluks," which are legendary for their warmth in the Arctic.

For Public Display
Maxine Belanger

On July 19, 1884, Maxine Belanger received Canadian Patent #19857 for a revolvingui device to display products.

Rachel Zimmerman had a terrific role model – her mom Linda, who was founder and president of her own software company.

"Women are generally more inventive. They notice more and make links between things."
Eugenia Kumacheva

A New Way of Communicating
Rachel Zimmerman

An interest in assistive technology led to a new communications tool. In the mid-1980s, thirteen-year-old Rachel Zimmerman from London invented a software program and adapted a special touch pad to greatly improve the communication abilities of people with physical disabilities such as cerebral palsy. Her invention is the BLISSYMBOL PRINTER. It is based on BLISSYMBOLICS, a communications system which was invented by Canadian Charles Bliss. BLISSYMBOLICS allows a person to communicate without using speech or writing. Symbols are featured on a board, and the user points to a symbol in order to express a message. Traditional BLISSYMBOLICS requires that someone be with the user at all times, to watch and interpret.

Rachel advanced this system further with the BLISSYMBOL PRINTER. Although the user still touches symbols on a special pad, now the chosen symbols are transformed into written language on a computer screen. The text can be read off a computer screen or printed on paper, in English or French. As Rachel said, "For people who can't read or write, this gives them a lot more independence." Her innovation won her the 1985 silver medal at the Canada-Wide Science Fair, and earned her a 1990 YTV (television) Youth Achievement Award. Rachel went on to study physics and space studies in university. Today, she works at The Planetary Society in California, teaching people about space exploration. Rachel is also interested in combining space and assistive technology, and her goal is to use NASA technologies to help people with disabilities.

Memory Power!
Eugenia Kumacheva

Dr. Eugenia Kumacheva, Associate Professor of Physical and Polymer Chemistry at the University of Toronto, is inventing a way for computers to hold more data than they currently do. Eugenia's invention would allow 10,000 gigs (roughly the amount of information stored on 14,286 CD Roms) of data to be stored on a computer chip the size of half a sugar cube.

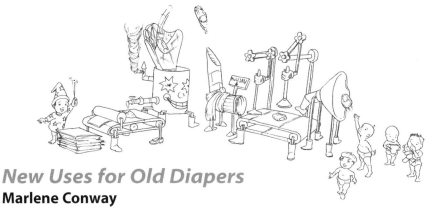

New Uses for Old Diapers
Marlene Conway

In 1950, American mom Marion Donovan made the first disposable diaper out of an old shower curtain and absorbent paper. Almost fifty years later, another mom, Marlene Conway of Toronto, invented a method to recycle more than five million disposable diapers thrown away annually in North America!

Though she didn't have a scientific background, Marlene's desire to help the environment inspired her to teach herself what she needed to know to invent the process. Her technology recycles both the absorbent material in the diaper and its waterproof cover. The first recycling demonstration facility using Marlene's technology opened in the mid-1990s in Ontario. The first full-scale commercial facility opened in Holland in 1999. Diapers come from sources such as hospitals, nursing homes and day care centres. Marlene holds more than ten patents on environment-related products or processes.

Marlene has become well-known as the "recycling lady." People are always mailing her used things they hope can be recycled. She says: "We have a ton of shoes, dishwasher racks, and other items. People will say to me 'Hey, is anyone dealing with this problem?'"

In 1996, the Chemical Institute of Canada presented Marlene with full Associate Degrees in Chemistry and Engineering for her achievements in environmental research.

Let's Play!
Laura Robinson

Sometimes, inventing means finding a new way of packaging a familiar idea. Actress Laura Robinson of London, and her friend Paul Toyne, took an old family game and turned it into the popular board game BALDER-DASH. In the game, players have to guess at finding the real meaning to obscure words, and try to outwit one another by creating bogus definitions. BALDERDASH is a hilarious test of creative wile. In 1987, it was the highest selling board game in Canada.

Look What's in a Disposable Diaper:

1) Polyethylene film for the back sheet prevents leaks.

2) Glue made from resins, oils, and tackifiers hold the diaper together.

3) Polypropylene resin material is used for the leg cuffs to prevent leaks.

4) Hydrophilic non-woven material is the main top inside surface. It lets liquids flow away from the baby into the diaper core.

5) Elastic made of polyurethane foam, rubber or stretchy plastic improves the fit.

6) Polypropylene and glue tabs keep the diaper on the baby.

7) Cellulose from pine trees makes the pad fluffy.

8) Polyacrilate is used in granular form in the pad so the diaper can hold more baby goo.

A Cleaner Environment
Dusanka Filipovic

Chemical Engineer Dusanka Filipovic has made ground-breaking discoveries and created important technologies that may help slow down the depletion of the earth's ozone layer.

While working for the Linde Division of Union Carbide Canada, Dusanka discovered that silicalite, a new zeolite adsorbent developed by Union Carbide, could recover CFCs, which are the main chemical ingredient in cooling appliances like refrigerators. CFCs can damage the earth's ozone layer when released into the earth's atmosphere. From 1986 to 1990, Dusanka developed a technology that could use silicalite for the large-scale recovery of CFCs. She called the technology BLUE BOTTLE.

The BLUE BOTTLE collects CFCs from refrigerators, air conditioners, and other equipment that are being repaired or have been abandoned. This is a critical time since CFCs often escape into the atmosphere from damaged or neglected devices. After the CFCs are collected, they are purified and reused in other industrial processes. In 1991, Dusanka left Linde to start her own company, Halozone. The company provides BLUE BOTTLES to customers such as major grocery chains, which use numerous freezers and coolers. Once a BLUE BOTTLE cylinder has been filled with CFCs by the customer, it is sent to Halozone's central reclamation facility where the CFCs are purified and transferred to storage containers. In 1993, Dusanka received the Manning Principal Award for Innovation, worth $100,000, for her invention of the BLUE BOTTLE.

In 1998, Dusanka started a new company, Blue-Zone Technologies Ltd., to apply the proven patented technology to the health science field. The technology reclaims and purifies valuable, unspent inhalation anaesthetic agents (greenhouse gases) that are routinely discharged into the atmosphere by hospitals. As well as helping to protect the environment, the technology also supplies hospitals with the highest quality USP grade anaesthetic agents, and in the most cost effective way. The technology is called DELTA, and it uses DELTASORB canisters. It is currently being demonstrated in Toronto with financial assistance from the National Research Council of Canada and Industry Canada.

Terrible Taste!
Great Mileage!
Inge Russell

Many inventions have been discovered by accident. Such was the case in the early 1980s, when a Canadian experiment to produce better beer surprisingly resulted in a new form of fuel alcohol for use in cars and machinery.

The inventor was Dr. Inge Russell of London, who was working as a Microbiologist at the Labatt Brewing Company. She extracted the genes from two different yeast strains (yeast is the main ingredient in beer), and combined them with a wax compound. The experiment yielded a new life-form, which she called "super yeast." Unfortunately, it made terrible tasting beer! Instead, it produced a powerful fuel alcohol, and at faster and greater quantity than previously known. Super yeast has found a growing market in several South American countries, including Brazil. Inge was the first person in Canada to receive a patent for a "laboratory constructed yeast for fuel ethanol production."

Inge is known around the world as an expert on yeast biotechnology. She has published 150 papers, reviews, and book chapters, and has written and edited various books on yeast biotechnology and brewing. She has been honoured with many awards including, in 2001, the YWCA Women of Distinction Award for Science & Technology. In recognition of her excellence in her field, Inge was recently nominated for membership in the prestigious Royal Society of Canada. Although newly retired, she continues to contribute to her profession as Editor of the *Journal of the Institute of Brewing*.

THE EYE MAKER Mirror
Colleen "Chips" Klein

Theatre performer Colleen "Chips" Klein of Toronto invented THE EYE MAKER mirror in the mid-1980s to solve a problem.

Flat theatre dressing room mirrors made it difficult for her to see her eyes from all angles, so applying make-up was a time-consuming task. Her solution was a mirror that makes the eye visible from all perspectives. Chips founded Chipco Canada Inc. to manufacture and distribute her invention. She has sold more than 500,000 worldwide.

"Don't give up. It's okay to fail a few times. Some of the most successful people failed many times. Failure results in opportunities for learning."
Inge Russell

Methanol and ethanol are two types of fuel alcohol used in cars. Ethanol can be produced from a variety of renewable resources, most commonly corn and sugarcane. Methanol can also be made from renewable resources, but today, methanol is primarily made from natural gas.

ideas · ingenuity · passion · creativity · inventiveness · inspiration

Manitoba

Look out upon our rolling prairies, carpeted with wild flowers and clotted over with poplar groves, where wild birds sing and chatter, and it does not seem too ideal or visionary that these broad sunlight spaces may be the homes of countless thousands of happy and contented people.

Nellie McClung, Author and Social Activist (1873-1951)
Excerpt from In Times Like These

The Staff of Life
Margaret Newton (1887-1971)

When we picture Manitoba, most of us think of endless fields of wheat. However, those wheat fields might not be there today were it not for the work of Dr. Margaret Newton.

In 1916, a terrible blight hit Canadian farms. The mysterious plant disease called "wheat rust" devastated wheat crops and nearly destroyed the grain industry overnight. Farmers were desperate and demanded that the Canadian government find a solution.

Fortunately, an undergraduate student at Montreal's McGill University found a way to keep the killer blight at bay. In 1917, Margaret Newton developed different varieties of wheat that were resistant to the rust. Not only did this send Canadian farming off on a new track, but it also set Margaret off on a career that would see her eventually become a world expert in plant pathology. Much of her research was carried out at the newly created Dominion Rust Research Centre in Winnipeg.

The first wheat grown in the west was planted in 1754 by Louis La Corne on the south shore of the North Saskatchewan River.

Margaret Newton was a determined young woman for her time. She continued with higher education despite her father's disapproval, eventually becoming, in 1922, the first Canadian woman to earn a Ph.D. in Agricultural Science. Unfortunately, Margaret's intensive work with rust spores damaged her lungs beyond repair, forcing her to retire in 1945. Today, she is fondly remembered as an important contributor to the development of Canada's large wheat industry. In 1992, twenty-one years after her death, Margaret was inducted into the newly created Science Hall of Fame in Ottawa.

Lotion for Beauty and Health
Lorraine Mignault

Cosmetics make us look good, but soon they may make us feel better too!

Inventor Lorraine Mignault of Winnipeg has spent twelve years researching and developing a formula for a personal-care therapeutic lotion. It can be used to both improve skin qualities, and treat health conditions such as headaches, insomnia, back pain, sports-related injuries, arthritis, and itching from various causes.

Made from all-natural ingredients, the lotion is called a "cosmeceutical" because it overlaps two areas – cosmetics and pharmaceuticals. In clinical trials, users reported that many health conditions were relieved and repaired. The lotion is not yet on the market, but should be in the near future, as an ingredient and as an end product via licensing of the worldwide patent pending technology. In 1999, Lorraine was a finalist in the Manitoba Woman Entrepreneur of the Year Awards, Innovation category. She was also published in the respected *Cosmetics & Toiletries®International Magazine* in April 2001.

Searching for Bugs
Diane Malley

Bugs and bacteria...watch out! A new super sleuth is making it possible to instantly locate and identify dangerous pollutants in soil and water. In 1991, Dr. Diane Malley of Winnipeg took an existing technology called Spectroscopy and began applying it to environmental analysis. Spectroscopy, which uses infrared light, had never before been used for this purpose. With it, soil and water samples are analysed in a minute or less. This is a huge improvement over other kinds of soil and water tests that can take weeks or months to complete. The speed and accuracy of the test allows quick action to be taken to avoid further damage to the environment, and to prevent illness in people and animals. This service is available through her company, PDK Projects Inc.

Diane has closely observed the serious problems faced by communities around the world when soil or water supplies are contaminated by hazards such as E. coli bacteria. As a result, Diane is committed to working towards making the world a better place.

Cosmetics have been worn throughout history by both women and men. For example, Cleopatra wore eyeliner and Louis XIV dusted his face with powder.

"Perseverance and a belief in one's abilities are important. Believing in yourself makes your work more credible."
Lorraine Mignault

"It is absolutely necessary to have worthy goals. Try to live your life so you can maximize a win-win situation. Consider learning a life-long process, and enjoy one's self."
Diane Malley

"The fun and excitement of inventing can be sustained only if someone else does the marketing."
Elaine Thompson

The Trans Canada Highway is the longest highway in the world. At 4,860 miles (7,821 km), it stretches from St. John's, Newfoundland, to Victoria, British Columbia. Now that's a lot of asphalt!

New Roads from Old Tires
Elaine Thompson

Instead of becoming a landfill problem, old tires can find new life on the highways they once travelled – all thanks to an invention by Dr. Elaine Thompson of Winnipeg.

Cold Canadian winters cause asphalt roads to crack. When this happens, not only do drivers have bumpy rides, but water soaks through the cracks, washing away the road below the surface. Prior to Elaine's invention, the only material available for the repair of road cracks was expensive, required specialized equipment for its application, and was dangerous to prepare and work with.

Elaine knew there had to be a better and less costly way to fix road cracks. After two years of research, she invented a process that recycles old rubber tires into asphalt emulsion, which can then be applied as a seal coat to road surfaces using conventional equipment. The rubber increases the flexibility of the seal coat and reduces the amount of cracking. The process is also good for the environment, since it helps solve the problem of how to dispose of used tires. Elaine received a patent for her invention in 1982.

Keeping Track of Mileage
Carolyn Gelhorn

For many people, such as taxi and truck drivers, their vehicle is their office. Just like regular businesses, these offices on wheels have to keep track of expenses and other data.

When Winnipeg sales manager Carolyn Gelhorn couldn't find a device to record her mileage, she invented one! The TRIPTRAC is an electronic device that is installed inside vehicles. It tracks mileage, the date and time of the trip, and gas purchases. The data can be printed using an internal paper supply within the TRIPTRAC, or downloaded into a personal computer. The TRIPTRAC eliminates the need for log books, and makes accounting easier for individuals and truck fleet owners. Carolyn spent five years developing the invention. She received a U.S. patent in 1985, and a Canadian patent two years later.

Baby Carrier Frees Hands
Judy Pettersen

Everyone knows babies like to be carried, but busy moms also need to have their hands free. In 1996, when Judy Pettersen couldn't find the perfect carrier for her fussy baby, she decided to invent her own. The BABYTREKKER carrier is designed for newborns to three-year-olds. Soft bodied and padded, babies can face in or out. It can also be worn in the front or on the back of the body.

The BABYTREKKER is a Manitoba success story. Judy struggled to find time to develop the carrier, while also caring for two children and expecting a third. But her efforts paid off. What started out as a business run out of Judy's kitchen now has its own manufacturing facility. The carrier is sold through her company, Pettersen Infant Products. In 1997, Judy received the Manitoba Home Business Woman of the Year award.

"Define who you are and what you want to be. Never accept other people's versions unless they encourage you."
Judy Pettersen

The Latest News
Ella Cora Hind (1861-1942)

Today, business people check the daily newspaper for the stock market report. In the early1900s, people in the business of farming frequently checked the crop report.

The crop report was invented by Manitoba trailblazer Ella Cora Hind. It became an important source of information for farmers, covering topics such as crop yields, livestock breeding, food production and marketing. Ella pioneered the use of crop reports while working as Commercial and Agricultural Editor for the *Winnipeg Free Press* newspaper, where she had started as a reporter in 1901. Her accurate agricultural analysis earned her worldwide recognition.

Ella Cora Hind was born in 1861 in Toronto, but moved to Winnipeg in 1882. Her life was a series of firsts. She was the first female journalist in western Canada, the first typist and stenographer, and the first woman to navigate a boat out of Manitoba's Port Churchill.

Kitchen Invention
Aganetta Peters

Like women of her time, much of Aganetta Peters' work revolved around food preparation. In 1920, she received Canadian Patent #195795 for a potato-preserving process that involved cutting potatoes, then sealing them in a salt water solution.

Saskatchewan

I long to hear the meadowlark
Sing my favourite prairie tune
And hold your hand dear,
'Neath that Saskatoon moon.

> Connie Kaldor, Singer and Songwriter
> *Song lyrics,* Saskatoon Moon

Plains First Nations People are credited with originating the name Saskatchewan. "Kisiskatchewan" means the river that flows swiftly – in reference to the most important waterway running through their territory.

Healthy Food for Babies

Deborah Haines

Newborn calves need mother's milk to survive. The first milk produced by the mother is called colostrum, which has a high concentration of antibodies. Antibodies are a substance produced by the body that destroy or render inactive certain diseases. Newborn calves use the antibodies in the colostrum to stay healthy, to fight disease, and to aid digestion.

In some cases, mother cows are unable to feed their calves and a colostrum substitute is needed. Veterinarian Dr. Deborah Haines of Saskatoon was concerned by the lack of high quality colostrum replacements for calves on the market. To remedy the problem, she invented HEADSTART. Since 1996, the colostrum replacement has been sold in Canada, Germany, Japan, and Mexico. Deborah is also developing colostrum for puppies, lambs, and aging house pets. Deborah says: "I am highly motivated by the thought I am benefitting the health of animals."

"The skills that are required to develop a successful small business are the same as those which many women use every day to organize the household and the social lives of a family."
Deborah Haines

Home Sewing Aid

Alice E. Grubb

A search at the Canadian patent office unearthed Canadian Patent #18330, which was issued on April 12, 1918 to Alice E. Grubb. The patent was for the HEM GAUGE, a tool that accurately measures and marks hemlines. Its design consists of a ruler device that attaches to the dress material. Although Alice remains a mystery, her invention reminds us that female inventors created products to make their work easier.

Cobalt 60 Therapy Unit
Sylvia Fedoruk

For more than fifty years, countless lives around the world have been saved because of a Canadian invention. The invention changed the way cancer was treated, giving people a chance at life.

In the early 1950s, as part of a four-person team led by Dr. Harold E. Johns at the University of Saskatchewan, young Sylvia Fedoruk helped to design and develop the Cobalt 60 Therapy Unit. It was the first cobalt machine to use radiation to treat cancer patients effectively. The machine took a radioactive source of cobalt and delivered it to patients using high intensity radiation. The first cancer patient treated with the Cobalt 60 Therapy Unit lived another fifty years and died only recently, well into her nineties.

Sylvia's measurement of the distribution of cobalt radiation as it penetrated the body (called isodose curves) allowed doctors to specify the dose of radiation the patient received. Sylvia also developed a scanning device that used radioactive iodine to determine whether or not a patient's thyroid was cancerous.

Sylvia has lived a vibrant life and received many honours. In 1961, she and her curling team won the first Canadian Women's Curling Championship. Sylvia also received many honourary university degrees and the Order of Canada. From 1986-1989, Sylvia also served as the Chancellor of the University of Saskatchewan. She crowned her long and distinguished career by serving as Lieutenant Governor of Saskatchewan from 1988-1994.

Pet Training Device

Marjorie Fehr

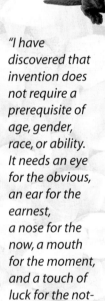

Aroma therapy for dog training? If you've ever tried to train a stubborn dog, you may be interested in a new invention by Marjorie Fehr of Martensville. At puppy school, Marjorie observed that her frisky puppy seemed more interested in the scent of the treat he was given to reinforce good behaviour than he was in its taste. He always seemed to be looking for something that smelled good. Marjorie enlisted the help of Donna M. Laye, a dog breeder and trainer. In 1999, they invented a scented pellet that could be used in dog training. The pellet can be placed in a variety of objects, such as a baton, to direct pet movements. It can also be tucked into food bowls to encourage stubborn pets to eat.

During the research and development stage, Marjorie and Donna were aided by a number of organizations that recognized tremendous potential in the product, including the Government of Canada through the Industrial Research Assistance Program. There is still a lot more work to be done before the pellet is available for sale. Presently, Marjorie and her partner are securing patents, exploring production options, and developing marketing strategies. Inventing has given Marjorie a tremendous sense of fulfilment and confidence. "It has encouraged me to think beyond the immediate," she says.

"I have discovered that invention does not require a prerequisite of age, gender, race, or ability. It needs an eye for the obvious, an ear for the earnest, a nose for the now, a mouth for the moment, and a touch of luck for the not-so-intrepid."
Marjorie Fehr

No More Needles

Marianna Foldvari

Thank goodness, no more needles! New ways of administering drugs are taking the "ouch" out of getting medicine.

Dr. Marianna Foldvari of Saskatoon has developed a new drug delivery system that replaces painful needles with patches and lotions. The medicine is encased in microscopic capsules that can be absorbed quickly and easily through the skin. Instead of an injection, a patient wears a prescribed patch, or applies a prescribed lotion or cream to treat illness. As President/Director of Research and Development of PharmaDerm Laboratories Ltd., Marianna has invented various other drug delivery systems. She has submitted sixteen patent applications for her inventions, and has been awarded six so far. In 1997, she received the YWCA Women of Distinction Award, Entrepreneur and Innovator Category.

Good Bugs!
Karen Lee Bailey

Even though you can't see them, "good bugs" may be a farmer's best friend! Dr. Karen Lee Bailey of Saskatoon specializes in the development of microscopic "bugs" (bacteria and fungi) to take over the role of pesticides in agriculture. Pesticides are presently used to prevent weed and bug damage to crops, but they are harmful to human beings and the environment, killing insects, plants and animals they were not meant to harm. The repeated use of pesticides can even result in the emergence of new "super bugs and weeds" that are resistant to the chemicals.

Karen works for Agriculture and Agri-Food Canada, where she conducts research in the emerging science of biotechnology. She has several patents pending for "bugs" she has developed for biological control. As well, she has identified new crop diseases in Canada and abroad, studied the impact of farming practices such as row spacing and crop rotation on crop yield, and registered new disease-resistant plant types. In the future, her research may benefit farmers economically and help to increase the world's food supply. Karen's philosophy about agriculture is also evident in her personal life. She and her husband operate an organic market garden to supply people with healthy food. She's a good cook, too!

New Therapies
Lillian Dyck

Many serious diseases attack the brain. Often, there is no cure. However, inquisitive researchers, with the help of new 21st century technologies, are unravelling some of the brain's secrets.

Dr. Lillian Dyck of Saskatoon is a Neuropsychiatry Researcher in the Department of Psychiatry at the University of Saskatchewan. She has developed and tested compounds which may one day help the body heal from neuro-degenerative disorders such as Parkinson's Disease, Alzheimer's Disease, and Multiple Sclerosis.

In 1996, Lillian developed a new class of beta-alanine compounds to treat various neuro-degenerative disorders. After extensive screening and experiments, she and her colleagues filed for a patent in 1998 and are awaiting finalization. Lillian's achievements were honoured in 1999, when she received a Science and Technology Award from the National Aboriginal Achievement Foundation.

Weeds are plants that grow where they are unwanted, in places like farmer's fields, lawns, and flower beds. Weeds cause damage by choking out desirable plants.

"Set your goals high, learn who you are. Set your own standards and never compromise yourself."
Karen Lee Bailey

"My inspirations are my mother – a Cree woman who died in 1956, my Cree spiritual heritage and feminist scientists"
Lillian Dyck

53

Alberta

Medical Breakthrough
Nora Dietlein

In 1967, a small group of British journalists in London, England gathered to watch a remarkable demonstration – a happy and very alive guinea pig completely submerged in water! A transparent silicone membrane surrounded the guinea pig. Through the membrane, oxygen and other gases passed freely, but water was kept out.

The membrane was much more than just a clever curiosity – it was medical breakthrough! The amazing material mimicked the alveolar membrane which separates blood and gases in the human lung. It was invented by Nora Dietlein, a University of Alberta graduate working on her doctorate in England.

The membrane was specifically designed for use in an artificial lung machine. Until Nora's invention, heart-lung machines allowed direct contact between the patient's blood and air, and that restricted their use to a few hours at most. The membrane led to the development of an oxygenator machine that could "breathe" for patients for up to twenty days. The oxygenator also made it possible for certain ill newborn infants to receive critical medical care shortly after birth instead of having to wait up to three weeks for their lungs to develop sufficiently. As well, the machine was used to transport organs for transplant procedures. Nora's membrane turned out to have many other medical applications. For example, it was the first artificial skin used to protect the flesh of burn victims.

A Good Night's Sleep
Gisele Jubinville

Gisele Jubinville of St. Albert is living proof that when it comes to inventing, persistence pays off. Gisele was convinced there had to be a better way to make fitted bed sheets so they didn't come untucked in the night. For two months, she sewed hundreds of designs, ignoring discouraging comments. One night, she awoke having dreamt of the perfect design. It used more fabric than normal, had a modified corner, and a unique seam that kept the sheet in place!

The hard work was not yet over. Gisele's patent application was rejected three times. Determined to prove her design unique, she went to Washington in 1994 where the American patent examiner approved her design. The following three years of production made it clear to Gisele that she couldn't compete with the big companies. But, instead of giving up, she sold her patent for $1 million U.S. to Springs Industries, an American sheet manufacturer. Today, Gisele is financially secure, and has the satisfaction of having fought for what she believed in. All for a good night's sleep!

Wired for Health
Elaine Murphy

Good health is just a pixel away. In 1991, Calgary veterinarian Dr. Elaine Murphy and her husband, physicist Robin Winsor, developed break-through technology for digital x-rays. The idea was born at a dinner party when discussion turned to the need for obtaining x-ray results faster. In three weeks, they built a rough prototype. Today, the digital x-ray machine, the IDC, is the basis of a company called Imaging Dynamics Inc. Units are now being installed in hospitals across the country.

An x-ray machine works by sending a beam of electrons toward a plate containing a layer of phosphorus and photographic film. When the beam hits the plate, the layer of phosphorus "lights up" and exposes the film. The IDC technology sends the image not to film, but to a digital camera, and then to a computer where the image can be manipulated. Compared to film, digital x-ray technology has proven to be faster, easier-to-store, and less expensive to use. The information is both sharper in resolution and more detailed than a traditional x-ray. An added bene-fit is that patients are exposed to radiation for shorter periods of time. A digital x-ray can be quickly sent to other computers, which allows doc-tors in different locations to see the same x-ray.

Curing by Stealth
Theresa Allen

Dr. Theresa Allen is using "Stealth" to outsmart a deadly enemy – cancer.

Certain kinds of cancers are treated by drugs that are carried to the affected area of the body in liposomes. Invented in the 1960s, liposomes are tiny, microscopic, soap-like bubbles that hold the cancer-fighting drugs. Unfortunately, sometimes the body's immune system detects the liposomes and rejects them as if they are a foreign invader, not a treatment, before they reach the tumor area. This renders the drugs useless.

In the 1990s, Theresa came up with an ingenious innovation to make liposomes more effective. She designed the liposomes with an outer layer similar to that of cells in the body (like red blood cells). This allows them to pass through the body undetected by the immune system. Like a fighter jet slipping by enemy radar, the liposomes can successfully reach their target and attack the cancerous tumour. The treatment was named after the Stealth Bomber, an aircraft that can avoid radar detection by the enemy!

Theresa says it is the scientist's job to be both prepared and open-minded; sometimes discoveries are made when ideas are put together. She was able to develop her innovation because the 1960s version of liposomes already existed. Now that she has discovered that liposomes can be disguised, the door is open for others to enhance and evolve this method of treatment.

"Keep an open mind to see where the opportunities are and at the same time pursue what's fun and interesting. Be willing to go out on a limb and question conventional wisdom. The truth does not always lie with what we already know."
Theresa Allen

Warm and Cosy Like a Womb
Carolyn Lawrence

The world can be a harsh place for premature babies. But Calgary's Carolyn Lawrence is helping to make their first weeks and months a little bit easier.

Carolyn has designed an incubator cover that reduces noise, dims light, and has an opening through which the baby's needs can be attended to by doctors and nurses. The cover also has pockets for stethoscopes and name cards. It can be used with Drager incubators and Air-Shield incubators. Another product developed by Carolyn is the SNUG-A-LOT wrap. The wrap helps support pre-term babies in a flexed position, as if they were still in their mother's womb. As well, she has created a tiny nightgown that snaps on easily.

In June 1995, Carolyn, with her mother-in-law, Anne Lawrence, started Smart Start Baby Boutique. Carolyn contracts stay-at-home moms to make her tiny creations. She sells her products over the Internet.

All of us started out in a womb where the environment is tightly controlled with little light and very little noise. These conditions are necessary since a baby needs protection for nine months. Even the smallest variation can cause shock to a tiny body.

Finding the Problem
Caroline Lai

In the finger-numbing sub-zero temperatures of a Canadian winter, a car that doesn't start can be a frustrating nuisance, as Electrical Engineer Caroline Lai of Edmonton found out. She was left stranded on a ski hill when her car wouldn't budge, despite being hooked up to a block heater to keep its engine warm.

Sometimes block heaters don't work. A block heater consists of a heating element that is inserted into the car's engine, and a power cord that plugs into an electrical outlet. Locating where the problem lies without some technical expertise or specialized equipment is difficult. Although a block heater can be checked at a garage, the test is costly.

In 1991, Caroline came up with an inexpensive solution that anyone can use. Her invention, PLUG ALIVE, is a palm-sized, easy-to-use device that plugs into either the block heater, the electrical outlet, or the extension cord. It indicates if power is present, and whether the block heater is working. Caroline manufactures and distributes PLUG ALIVE through her company, Yoken Inc. More than ten thousand units have been sold. PLUG ALIVE is also useful in industries such as construction, where it can be used to identify electrical problems. Caroline says that inventing has taught her that she can achieve anything she desires.

British Columbia

The sun enriched the old poles grandly. They were carved elaborately and with great sincerity. Several times a woman that held a child was represented. I sat in front of a totem mother and began to draw.

Emily Carr, Artist (1871-1945)
Diary excerpt

Lights...Action
Royann Petrell

Feed your fish right and it just might be your friend for life. A well-cared-for goldfish can live to be seventy years old!

If you've ever owned pet fish, you know how hard it is to feed them just the right amount. Imagine how hard it must be for a fish farmer, with thousands of fish to feed!

Now, a new invention called AQUAMON lets fish farmers know when the fish have had a sufficient amount of food. The inventor is Dr. Royann Petrell of Vancouver, who is a Professor of Chemical and Biological Engineering at the University of British Columbia. AQUAMON consists of an underwater camera and computer programming. It automatically checks for uneaten pellets and signs of fish feeding, and can be used to adjust feeding discharge rates. The device has a direct application on "in net" cages of salmon farms that contain up to thirty-thousand fish each. Royann has also invented VICASS (Video Imaging Capturing and Sizing System), which collects data on how schools of fish move within an enclosed space, and how big the fish are without taking them out of the water. The high definition, real-time visual image also records information such as the general health of the fish and how fast they are swimming.

Royann's fish imaging laboratory at the university is a busy place. She has several other projects on the go, as well as a patent pending for an enhanced fish pellet (fish food). One of her graduate students is developing a novel method to trap the waste particles from a salmon farm, while another student is developing a biosensor for detecting the dissolved material. Both inventions (if proven effective) will be used by fish farmers to ensure that their farms are not negatively affecting the environment.

New Computer Language
Veronica Dahl

In the future, it may be possible to carry on a conversation with your computer. Dr. Veronica Dahl of Port Moody helped develop an entirely new programming language that has brought human and computer language a big step closer.

Veronica is a Professor of Computer Sciences at Simon Fraser University. Fuelled by a desire to bridge the gap between the science of language (linguistics) and the science of computers, she helped develop LOGIC PROGRAMMING, an active area in computing sciences. She pioneered its use for processing natural language, describing knowledge bases, and extracting information from raw text documents.

Computer programmers use code to communicate to the computer what they want it to do. LOGIC PROGRAMMING code is more readable by non-computer specialists, being based on logic. Veronica was recognized by the Association of Logic Programming as one of the founders of the field, along with 13 other international scientists.

Young Inventor
Gina Gallant

Gina Gallant of Prince George has definitely caught the invention bug!

When Gina was twelve years old, her little brother was involved in a serious bicycle accident. Luckily, he only received a mild concussion thanks to a properly worn bicycle helmet. But the incident made her think about how many children wear their helmets improperly – too loosely or too far back on the head.

She spent three hundred hours designing a "smart" bicycle helmet. A series of sensors inside the helmet activate lights on the outside of the helmet when it is worn properly. Her invention has attracted a lot of attention. Gina even reached the semi-finals in the YTV (television) Youth Achievement Awards!

Her second invention is a recipe for crackers that stay crunchy longer in soup. As well, she is currently researching methods of combining plastics recovered from landfill sites with asphalt to create PAR - Paving Our Future (PAR is an abbreviation for PolyAggreRoad).

"Time is your most valuable resource. It is the material from which life is made. Don't squander it in pursuits that are truly not yours, or in any kind of negativity. Dream, dare and imagine. Aim high, even impossibly high. Good by-products will come out of trying."
Veronica Dahl

59

Smart Steel
Indira Samarasekera

Thanks to the work of Dr. Indira Samarasekera, the cars we ride in have a better chance of staying intact if they are in an accident.

Indira is a Materials Engineer and Professor at the University of British Columbia. She has created mathematical models to predict the mechanical properties of hot rolled steel. In this process, "artificial intelligence" is added to steel mills in the form of information. Sensors allow the machine operators to see and correct defects in the process of "continuous steel coating" at every moment of production.

Eliminating defects during the steel coating process is crucial because defects can decrease the strength of steel. For instance, the body of a car made of steel with a defect is more vulnerable to fracturing than a car body without the defect.

No More Allergic Reactions
Helen Burt

A challenging dilemma required an innovative solution. Paclitaxel is a cancer fighting drug which has shown promise in fighting inflammatory diseases such as Rheumatoid Arthritis, Multiple Sclerosis, and Psoriasis. However, one of the ingredients in the injectable form of paclitaxel caused an allergic reaction in some people.

In 1993, Dr. Helen Burt, a Pharmaceutical Sciences Professor at the University of British Columbia, set out to find an answer to the dilemma. Her goal was to create an injectable form of paclitaxel without the problem of allergic responses. Because paclitaxel did not dissolve in water, designing a new injectable, water-based formulation was a challenge. Her solution – a biodegradable plastic bubble to hold the medicine. The bubble has two functions: to bind its oily-like interior to the paclitaxel, and to carry the ingredient into the body. As a result of Helen's tiny bubbles, the water solubility of the paclitaxel increased five thousand times, making it suitable for injection.

Helen is the inventor of several filed and granted patents for her work, developing new and better ways to deliver drug treatments to the body.

PINE-O-MITE Fire Starter!
Liana Greiner

When it comes to lighting creative fires, Liana Greiner is an expert.

In 1999, Liana invented the PINE-O-MITE, an inexpensive and effective homemade fire starter. At the time, Liana was a grade seven Okanagan Valley student looking for a good idea for her science fair project. She didn't have to look far. The ground outside her house was covered with fallen pine needles and cones, which she believed could be recycled into a useful product. Liana successfully combined the materials with recycled dryer lint, cardboard tubing from toilet paper and Christmas wrapping, and paraffin wax to create the PINE-O-MITE. Resembling a small stick of dynamite, the fire starter ignites quickly, and burns even when wet! When broken in half, each half burns for twenty-five minutes.

The innovative use of local, recycled materials in the PINE-O-MITE has earned Liana many science fair awards. Liana hopes to one day market the PINE-O-MITE through the Internet.

Needles and pine cones are a fire hazard because they ignite easily when exposed to a spark. They contain a natural fluid that acts as a fuel. Some forest fires actually help the natural forest growth cycle as the fires clear out older decayed trees and give new young trees the room and sunlight they need to grow.

Sharp Television
Rabab Ward

You can thank Dr. Rabab Ward when your favourite television shows arrive from the studio to your TV set with picture-perfect clarity.

Rabab is a Professor of Electrical Engineering at the University of British Columbia. Her desire to design better operational systems for televisions led her to invent low cost software that reduces video noise in analog and digital television signals, making the picture quality better. Rabab has received three patents for her invention, the Signal Quality Monitoring System, which allows cable companies to detect problems with television signals.

Robot Power!
Elizabeth Croft

Want your robot to be a smooth operator? Call Dr. Elizabeth Croft.

Elizabeth is an Associate Professor in the Department of Mechanical Engineering at the University of British Columbia. She creates algorithms that are the basis for motion generation software for industrial robots. Elizabeth's algorithms allow for smooth robotic movement, so that robots move with less jerking and greater precision. The robots could be used for surgery and other practices which require very precise movements.

"Work towards it, believe it, and work hard. Pay attention to your body, soul and mind. The three work together."
Rabab Ward

Hips and Knee Joints
Nancy Paris-Seeley

Bio-medical Engineer Nancy Paris-Seeley of Vancouver loves the process of taking a new concept all the way from the idea stage through to the clinical trial stage. That's a good thing for us, since Nancy's ideas help improve people's lives.

She is the inventor of numerous new medical products for the health-care industry. One product measures the success of shoulder surgery. Other products include dramatically improved artificial hip and knee joints. These joints are superior to the ones previously used for hip and knee replacements. The old-style joints often became infected, sometimes leaving patients bedridden for prolonged periods of time. Nancy is also working on a new and better method of removing stents (devices which hold tissue in place) from children.

"Risk-taking is something women should do more often."
Nancy Paris-Seeley

Nancy's work has made her a "very happy person." She is passionate about her profession, and believes that engineering can help advance the medical field.

Jolly Jumper
Olivia Poole

Olivia Poole proves the old adage that "necessity is the mother of invention." In the early 1950s, Olivia was a mother of seven young children, and at her wits end trying to keep the baby happily occupied. One day, she remembered something she had seen as a young girl growing up on the White Earth Indian Reservation in Minnesota. There, traditional cradle boards were suspended from tree branches by leather straps, letting babies bounce contentedly.

During athletic activity, the knee experiences strong, sudden forces. As a result, knee injuries are one of the most common types of athletic injuries.

Olivia rigged up her own contraption from a broom handle, fabric, and a coiled spring. Thus, the JOLLY JUMPER was created. Olivia, and her husband Joseph, started manufacturing the JOLLY JUMPER after they moved to British Columbia. By 1959, several thousand per month were being produced at their North Vancouver factory. Since then, parents around the world have used the JOLLY JUMPER to quiet and entertain babies, providing parents with a much-needed moment of peace.

The Gift of Sight
Julia Levy

Dr. Julia Levy of Vancouver is on the cutting-edge of one of the most exciting new areas in medicine. She is known worldwide as a pioneer in the field of Photodynamic Therapy (PDT) – a medical field using light-activated drugs to treat diseases.

With PDT, patients are injected with a specially tailored drug, which enters the bloodstream and concentrates itself in the diseased area of the body. The drug is then activated with laser light, allowing it to attack the diseased area.

Julia is a Microbiology Professor at the University of British Columbia. She is also co-founder, President and CEO of the biotechnology company, QLT Photo Therapeutics Inc. Two of the therapies developed by QLT – PHOTOFRIN and VISUDYNE – are effectively treating cancers and eye conditions, including a form of the devastating eye disease AMD (age-related macular degeneration).

VISUDYNE was a personal triumph for Julia, whose mother lost her vision as a result of AMD. "Being part of a team that will change the world for thousands of people, by enabling them to maintain their vision as they get older, has made me feel very lucky," she says.

No More Wrinkles!
Antoinette Goldschmidt

In 1878, Antoinette Goldschmidt received Canadian Patent #9363 for her invention of an improved ironing board. It was designed with adjustable wooden sections that fit specific types of garments.

Posters, Anyone?
Ethel Girling Clark

Hanging posters without damaging them is always a challenge. In 1936, Ethel received Canadian Patent #355969 for her invention of a hanging system that eliminates pinning and taping. Posters are laid on a cloth roller device that catches the top and bottom of the poster. The device is then attached to the wall.

"There is an saying 'Luck favours the prepared mind.' I know this to be the case in my life, so my advice is to keep your peripheral vision active at all times. You never know when events will unfold which can dramatically change the course of your life."
Julia Levy

A form of AMD (called wet AMD) is the leading cause of blindness in the elderly. It causes a loss of central vision, resulting in a severe reduction in the quality of life for patients as their ability to read, watch television, drive, and even see the faces of their loved ones is diminished.

The North

Yukon, Nunavut, Northwest Territories

And this is the community feast. You see there, part of that house showing, that is the Community Hall, and all the rest are Native houses. In those days, there was no traffic of any kind. On our feet, we wore moccasins made of moosehide. Fort McPherson's ground was good green grass. So instead of staying inside, everyone sat outside on the grass.

Sarah Simon, Linguist (1901-2001)
Excerpt from Sarah Simon: A Pictorial Account of Family, Church and Community

The invention of the parka ensured survival in the bitter cold of the Arctic. Traditional parkas always had hoods and were made either of seal skin, or caribou hide. Women's parkas had larger hoods than men's because they carried babies on their backs inside the hoods.

Native Technology

The bitterly cold climate of the Canadian North, where winter temperatures in some areas can fall as low as -40°C, molded every aspect of life and set the stage for innovation. The original native inhabitants used local resources to ensure survival. Native technologies of all kinds were made out of natural materials. Animal bones were turned into tools, animal skin became clothing, and snow and ice were used as building materials to create shelters such as igloos. It is likely that native women invented or improved many of the native technologies, particularly those used in cooking, skin tanning and making clothing, since they generally performed these tasks.

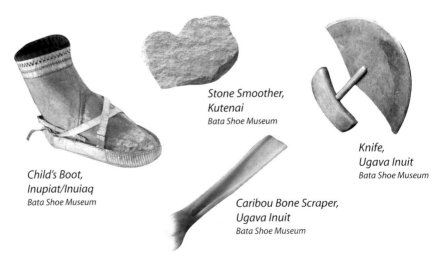

Stone Smoother, Kutenai
Bata Shoe Museum

Knife, Ugava Inuit
Bata Shoe Museum

Child's Boot, Inupiat/Inuiaq
Bata Shoe Museum

Caribou Bone Scraper, Ugava Inuit
Bata Shoe Museum

64

Yukon

Culture Through Dance
Clara Schinkel

Preserving dying cultural traditions requires innovative thinking!

In the 1970s, Clara Schinkel from Whitehorse was concerned by the Native people's loss of culture. In her hometown, the use of traditional languages such as Tlingit and Tagish had greatly decreased. Clara decided to use traditional songs and dances as a tool to preserve the culture. She believed that through singing and dancing, children and adults could learn their people's language, stories, and history.

In 1973, Clara started the Carcross-Tagish Dancers group with just a handful of children. Today, the group has more than forty dancers ranging in age from babies as young as eight months old to elders nearing eighty. The dance group has spread knowledge about Native culture throughout the world, having danced in countries as far away as Japan and Russia. Most importantly, the dance group offers children in the community an opportunity to gain knowledge and an appreciation for their heritage.

"Know yourself, know your history, and take pride in your identity."
Clara Schinkel

Yukon

New Way of Storytelling
Louise Profeit-Leblanc

In the Yukon, storytelling has emerged once again as a powerful voice of the people.

In June 1987, innovator Louise Profeit-Leblanc co-founded the first Yukon International Storytelling Festival. As well, she is developing a new approach to storytelling in which a traditional Native story is first introduced in kindergarten and, in each subsequent grade, students study the story in greater depth. Through the story, students are introduced to the traditional symbols and metaphors of Yukon First Nations mythology. By grade twelve, the students will have learned the true meaning of the story, and how to apply the knowledge they have gained to their own lives.

"Recognize that you should try to help others. It's your job. Making others happy makes you happy."
Louise Profeit-Leblanc

Louise calls herself an Engineer because she builds bridges between people. She is a member of the Nacho-N'Yak Dun (People of the Big River) First Nation in the Northern Yukon (from the Mayo region). Her work in the area of mental health, specifically suicide prevention, was the reason why she got involved in arts and heritage preservation. She believes that through knowing and practicing one's culture, future generations will be happy and healthy, both mentally and spiritually.

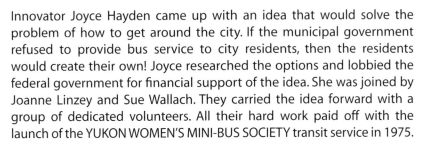

Yukon

Ride, Anyone?

Joyce Hayden

"Attitude is everything – don't give up. The greatest disability is low self-esteem."
Joyce Hayden

In the early 1970s, the Yukon city of Whitehorse was widely spread out but lacked public transit. Most families could only afford one vehicle and many mothers of young children battled "cabin fever," particularly during the long, bitterly cold winter months. Teens and children often had to hitchhike to their after-school activities, sports events, movie theatres, and restaurants. The elderly and the poor were also affected by the lack of public transit. In spite of the demand, the municipal government deemed a transit system unnecessary.

Innovator Joyce Hayden came up with an idea that would solve the problem of how to get around the city. If the municipal government refused to provide bus service to city residents, then the residents would create their own! Joyce researched the options and lobbied the federal government for financial support of the idea. She was joined by Joanne Linzey and Sue Wallach. They carried the idea forward with a group of dedicated volunteers. All their hard work paid off with the launch of the YUKON WOMEN'S MINI-BUS SOCIETY transit service in 1975.

For many Yukon women this was their first opportunity to work in a non-traditional job with flexible hours. Women did the driving, cleaning, repairing, accounting, and promotion. They worked hard to cut costs, improve service, and keep the buses rolling.

The bus service was a tremendous success. The system began as a phone-in service that also ran some regular schedules. People were picked up and dropped off at their own door, or they could flag down a bus along the streets and highways. Ridership grew and, in 1978, the municipal government took over the system. In 1999, Joyce Hayden was named the Yukon Transportation Hall of Fame's Person of the Year in recognition of the unique start and service of the YUKON WOMEN'S MINI-BUS SOCIETY.

Nunavut
Earth Paper
Cyndi Foster and
Students from Kullik School

If you live in the Arctic, what would you do with muskox poop? Why, make paper, of course!

In Cambridge Bay, one of Canada's most northern towns, paper rescued from recycling bins is combined with an unusual ingredient – re-hydrated muskox poop – to create an environmentally-friendly hand-made paper called EARTH PAPER. The inventors are teacher Cyndi Foster and the elementary students from Kullik School.

Paper is made from fibres that come from trees or other plants. Since a muskox is a plant eating animal, its diet is a gold mine of fibres that can be harvested at the end of the digestive process. As well, the kind of plants the muskox eats produces strong, woody fibres, which are perfect for making strong sheets of paper. The muskox's stomach acids are also very effective in breaking down the plant bits into fibres. EARTH PAPER is slightly thicker than commercial paper. Plant material flecks are visible throughout the sheet and the surface is slightly textured.

What originally started as an art experiment has attracted much local and national interest. The Nunavut government even purchased paper to give as gifts to the Members of the Legislature and Ministers. Students presented the gifts during the May 2001 Legislature sessions. The recent addition of a solar panel has turned the school into an environmentally-friendly paper mill. Students use solar power to run the electrical equipment, however, the solar panel can only operate during the summer when light is available for twenty-four hours each day, not in the winter when it is dark even in the daytime. Papermaking takes place during art class, sometimes after school and on the occasional weekend. The paper is sold locally to community members.

Covered with a thick coat to protect against bitter Arctic weather, the herbivore muskox roam the tundra of the Arctic mainland and the Arctic islands. Though they resemble bison, muskox are related to goats, sheep and cows.

Paper was invented in China in 600 B.C. Each hand-made sheet was made from plant material that was pounded into pulp. This released the plant's fibres, which were then floated in water. Papermakers formed sheets of paper by dipping wooden screens into the water and capturing the fibres as the screen was lifted up.

1

2

3

4

DONE!

Northwest Territories

Artist: Elisapee Itulu

Artists Get Together
Charlene Alexander

The artists of the Northwest Territories were desperately in need of a way to connect with each other. They were isolated from one another in communities that were hundreds, and even thousands, of miles apart.

It took an innovative idea to bridge the distances. In 1989, Charlene Alexander came up with a creative solution to the problem – an art festival. Charlene, who is also an artist, worked at an art gallery in Inuvik. She saw how difficult it was for artists to meet, and how it was almost impossible for artists to travel to see their work displayed in exhibitions. With Sue Rose, she co-founded The Great Northern Arts Festival.

The annual Great Northern Arts Festival non-profit event has become the gathering point for artists from the Northwest Territories, as well as the Yukon and Nunavut. Artists from far-flung communities are able to meet, share techniques, get marketing tips, and inspire each other. The artists represent all northern cultures: Inuvialuit, Gwich'in, Dene, Inuit, Athapaskan, Metis, and non-aboriginal. They work in all media, ranging from traditional carving to contemporary printmaking. When the festival began, it was attended by only a handful of artists. Now, more than eighty artists participate yearly. Sponsorship funding from a variety of sources makes it possible for artists to make the journey. The Great Northern Arts Festival is held in Inuvik for ten days at the end of July. Inuvik is the most northerly community in North America accessible by public road.

"Work through an idea from as many angles as possible before moving onto the next idea."
Charlene Alexander

Northwest Territories

Looking Good
Isabella Cornell

On February 12th, 1885, Isabella Cornell received Canadian patent #21089 for a complexion-improving cosmetic.

Northwest Territories

Preserving a Language
Sarah Simon (1901-2001)

For much of her life, Sarah Simon acted as a gateway between the English and Gwich'in worlds. Born near Fort McPherson, Sarah was a much revered and loved elder within her community. At the age of ninety, she was awarded the Order of Canada in recognition of her many years of service to her church and community.

The award stated: "She has spent her lifetime preserving and promoting the culture of the Loucheux (old French term for Gwich'in) people. She is a skilled linguist whose dedicated work as a translator and interpreter ensured that her people's needs were met and understood by the many officials who visited the northern communities over the years." Sarah made cassette tape recordings of the Bible, Prayer Book, and Hymnal using the Gwich'in language. She also delivered eighty-five babies. Sarah lived to be one hundred years old.

The Gwich'in Athapaskan language has also been known as Loucheux, Kutchin and Tukudh. It is spoken in northern Yukon, northeast Alaska and in the northwest corner of the Northwest Territories.

Northwest Territories

Northern Fashion
Berna Beaulieu

The Northwest Territories has emerged as a place of fashion. Clothing design that combines traditional aboriginal motifs and materials, such as caribou hide, with contemporary design is causing people to take notice.

Designer Berna Beaulieu of Yellowknife is a member of the Dogrib Rae First Nation. In 1997, Berna started her company, Creations by Berna, when she realized that the traditional designs of her people were gradually dying off with the older generation. She hopes to help preserve her culture through her clothing design. Berna's fashions – each vest, dress, shirt and motif – are one of a kind. Her clothing can be seen on the dance floor and in government.

In 1997, Berna had the honour of presenting the Premiers of Canada with caribou hide vests. Recently, she presented traditional 3/4-length jackets and vests to the Speaker of the House and Clerks of the Legislative Assembly of the Northwest Territories. In 1999, Berna received the People's Choice and Artist Choice Awards from The Great Northern Arts Festival.

"I believe each and every one of us has a God given talent and a lifetime to achieve it. Be patient and in the end you'll come out a winner."
Berna Beaulieu

ideas • ingenuity • passion • creativity • inventiveness • inspiration

Let's Invent!

Every inventor invents in her or his own special way, but there are certain steps that simplify the invention process.

1) IDENTIFY THE PROBLEM!

Avoid creating a solution until you have identified the problem.

2) RESEARCH!

Gather as much information as possible on the problem. The more you know, the better the solution. If you would like to sell your invention, ask friends and family if they would buy something that solves the problem and, if so, how much they'd be willing to pay for it.

3) DOES A SOLUTION ALREADY EXIST?

Go to the Canadian patent office web site (www.cipo.gc.ca) to find out if someone has already invented a solution to the problem. If an invention already exists, you can design something that you think will work even better, or move on to another problem.

4) WHAT WILL YOUR INVENTION DO?

Figure out the tasks that the invention is expected to perform, and the characteristics in the final design that will enable the invention to complete the tasks. Number them in order of importance. Focus on meeting the highest ranking ones.

5) LET YOUR IMAGINATION GO!

Brainstorm as many ideas as possible to solve the problem. Next, turn these ideas into designs. No matter how bizarre or unrealistic a design may seem, make sure to write it down, or sketch it out. Although a design may seem impossible, it might inspire a realistic solution.

6) NARROW IT DOWN!

Analyze your designs based on cost, efficiency, and other factors such as appeal for the intended user. Refine your final design, and prepare working drawings. The drawings should feature two to three different views that provide relevant information of the design. Draw the designs to scale, and write down the actual dimensions.

PATENTS

Inventors apply to the government for a patent. The inventor agrees to reveal information about the invention to the public and, in return, the government grants the inventor the exclusive right to make and sell the invention for a specific period of time.

COPYRIGHT

Creative products like books and paintings are legally protected by copyright. Unlike patents, getting a copyright is very easy and free. All you do is place the copyright © symbol with your name and date on all things that you create.

7) MAKE IT REAL!

Make a prototype (model) based on your working drawings. Figure out how you can use existing knowledge and materials for the prototype. Once you have completed your prototype, experiment with it.

8) NAME YOUR INVENTION!

Have fun. You can name it to describe what the invention does, name it after yourself, or you can just make the name up. Make sure the name is unique and memorable.

9) PROTECT YOUR IDEA!

Patents and trademarks are granted by the government and give owners the right to be the only maker and seller of the invention for a specific time period. Since the patent process is costly, avoid applying for a patent until you know that you will be able to sell your invention.

10) FINE TUNING IT!

Perfect the look of the invention. Often, inventors hire a specialist such as an industrial designer to help them do this.

11) FINANCING!

If you think that your invention is going to be a hit, it will cost a lot of money to get it ready for future sales. You can check out banks for assistance, or you can ask your family or friends if they would like to invest in your venture.

12) MAKING MANY COPIES!

Figure out how best to manufacture the invention. Does it have to be made in a factory? Manufacturing involves taking the working drawings, and using them to produce a large quantity of the invention.

13) FINDING A CUSTOMER!

After all your hard work, you want to make sure your invention has customers. This stage of the invention process is called "marketing." You will need to design an attractive package, create advertising, talk to store buyers and potential customers, and more!

Did you have any idea that there were so many things to think about? Often, inventors sell their idea directly to companies who are set up to do all these steps. The inventor then receives a one-time fee, a percentage of future sales, or sometimes both.

TRADE SECRETS
Shhh…don't tell anyone. Not all great ideas are patented. Some inventors decide they can get better protection by keeping their invention secret. The formula for COCA COLA™ is believed to be locked in a bank vault.

TRADEMARKS
Take a look around you. Labels and well-known brands are everywhere. For example, everyone is familiar with Roots™ sweat shirts and Apple™ computers. The ™ stands for trademark and the ® for a trademark that has been formally registered with the federal government. A trademark protects the name of the product, not the product itself.

Canadian Men Invent!

Canadian men are responsible for a vast number of inventions we recognize and use everyday. From food to sports, machines to games, their inventions reflect and illuminate the times in which they lived. Like every inventor, they asked "What if?" So, who are they?

Telephone, 1876

"Watson! Come here, I need you," said Alexander Graham Bell to his assistant Watson. These were the first words ever spoken using the telephone. Bell is known around the world as the inventor of the telephone. At the time, he was just twenty-nine years old. In 1877, he formed the Bell Telephone Company. A prolific inventor, Bell patented eighteen inventions of his own and another twelve with colleagues. His inventions include the hydrofoil boat, the telegraph, and the phonograph.

Time Zones, 1885

Today, the invention of time zones by Sir Sandford Fleming allows us to know the exact time anywhere in the world. Until one hundred years ago, most communities figured it was noon when the sun was overhead, so time varied from town to town. In 1879, Fleming suggested that the world should be divided into twenty-four equal time zones, with a standard time in each zone. In 1883, all North American railway companies adopted his idea and by 1885, Greenwich Mean Time (GMT) was established. This placed England as the place where time starts.

Superman, 1938

Faster than a speeding bullet! Joe Shuster, an artist for the Toronto Star Newspaper, and American Jerome Siegel, were the creators of SUPERMAN. The comic first appeared in June 1938. Shuster & Siegel sold their character to DC Comics in 1940. Superman is the first and most famous of the "super heros."

5 Pin Bowling, 1909

Thomas F. Ryan invented 5-pin bowling in the early 1900s. This distinctly Canadian form of bowling is enjoyed across Canada by over one million people in more than seven hundred bowling centres.

Pablum, 1920s

Creamy baby food PABLUM, the first pre-cooked, vitamin-enriched cereal, was invented by doctors Alan Brown, T.G.H. Drake, and Frederick F. Tisdall who worked at the Hospital for Sick Children in Toronto. The name comes from "pabulum," a Greek word for food.

Snowmobile, 1922

Joseph-Armand Bombardier of Valcourt, Quebec was just fifteen years old when he invented the first snowmobile by attaching a propeller to an automobile engine, which he then mounted on an old sleigh. In 1922, he arrived at a design that became the basis of today's snowmobile.

Basketball, 1891

James Naismith of Almonte, Ontario invented the game of basketball in 1891. His intent was to provide an indoor activity for a rowdy class of students. He wrote down the first set of game rules in 1892. These rules are virtually unchanged today. In 1959, Naismith was inducted into the Basketball Hall of Fame, which opened that same year.

Hockey Mask, 1950s

He shoots, he scores! Hockey legend Jacques Plante designed the first-ever fibreglass hockey mask as a result of his dangerous profession as goalie for the *Montreal Canadiens* hockey team (1954-1963). Today, the hockey mask is used throughout all hockey leagues worldwide.

Odometer, 1854

The invention of the odometer was a first in 1854. Samuel McKeen of Nova Scotia thought to attach a device to the wheel of a carriage, thereby measuring the total distance travelled.

And the list goes on...

McIntosh Apple

Insulin

Lacrosse

Frozen Food

Gingerale

Canadarm

Steam Foghorn

Panoramic Camera

Electron Microscope

Zipper

Paint Roller

Green Ink

Hydrofoil Boat

Blissymbolics

Documentary Films

73

Index

Index

Index

ingenuity • passion • creativity • inventiveness • inspiration

Sources

Abbott, Maude - Quebec
The Gazette, Montreal, March 13,
2000: Assistant Prof Who Was
Known World Over.
MacDermot, H.E., Maude Abbott: a
Memoir, 1941.
Canadian Medical Association,
1990: Dr. Maude Abbott Deserves
Better.

Adams, Ruth - Ontario
Letters: Ruth Adams to the
Administrator of the Government
of the Province of Canada: June 7,
1854; July 20, 1854; July 21, 1854.
Letters: Crown Law Department of
Quebec to Ruth Adams: January
20, 1855; July 28, 1854.
Agricultural Office, 1854, no. 293.

Ann Vare, Ethlie & Ptacek, Greg,
Mothers of Invention: From the Bra
to the Bomb: Forgotten Women &
Their Unforgettable Ideas, Quill
William Morrow, New York, 1989.

Alexander, Charlene
IW Interview, Summer, 2000.
www.greatart.nt.ca/partners.htm

Allen, Theresa - Alberta
IW Interview, Summer, 2000.
Folio, University of Alberta,
September, 1998.
Canadian Patent Database.

Bailey, Karen Lee - Saskatchewan
IW Interview, Summer, 2000.
Pimentel, D, Techniques for
Reducing Pesticide Use. John Wiley
& Sons Ltd., New York, 1997.
Agriculture and Agri-Food Canada
Research Branch, June, 2000.

Bell, Mabel - Nova Scotia
Carpenter, Thomas, Inventors:
Profiles in Canadian Genius: Mabel
Bell and the Aerial Experiment
Association; Kites, Wings and
Flight. Camden House Publishing,
Camden, 1990.
Eber, Dorothy, Genius at Work,
Images of Alexander Graham Bell.
McClelland & Stewart Ltd.,

Toronto,1982.
Toward, Lilias M., Mabel Bell,
Alexander's Silent Partner.
Methuen Publications, Agincourt,
1984
Green, Gordon H., The Silver Dart,
Brunswick Press Ltd., Fredericton,
1959.

Beaulieu, Berna - Northwest
Territories
IW Interview, Summer, 2000.
The Yellowknife, March 8, 2000.

Briand, Micheline - Prince Edward
Island
IW Interview, Summer, 2000.
The Guardian Newspaper,
Charlottetown, April 1, 2000.

Brodie, Beverly - Prince Edward
Island
Canadian Trade-Marks Database.

Caney, Steven, Steven Caney's
Invention Book. Workman
Publishing Company Inc., New
York, 1985.

Casey, Susan. Women Invent: Two
Centuries of Discoveries That have
Shaped Our World. Chicago Review
Press, Chicago, 1997.

Chan, Catherine - Prince Edward
Island
IW Interview, Summer, 2000.
Guardian Newspaper,
Charlottetown, Diabetes
Supplement, November 6, 1997:
Federal Court Awards Patent for
Lab Mouse.

Conway, Marlene - Ontario
IW Interview, Summer, 2000.
Conway, M. & Anderson, W., PLCAO
Sodium Polyacrylates in
Horticulture.
Canadian
Business,September,1996.

Cook, Sharon Anne, Framing Our
Past: Canadian Women's History in
the Twentieth Century.
McGill-Queens University Press.

Cornell, Isabella - Northwest
Territories
Canadian Patent Database.

Daley, Carole - New Brunswick
IW Interview, Summer, 2000.

Dietlein, Nora - Alberta
New Trail Alumni Magazine,
University of Alberta, Winter, 1999.

Devost Reckler, Lise - New
Brunswick
IW Interview, Summer, 2000.
Eureka: The Canadian Invention
and Innovation Newsletter,
Summer, 1997.

Dicks, Alice - Newfoundland
IW Interview, Summer, 2000.
Canadian Living, April, 1997.

Dunn-Pickard, Colleen -
Newfoundland/Labrador
IW Interview, Fall, 2001.
Department of Development and
Rural Renewal, Human Resources
Development Canada.
www.gmo.nf.ca/motherrnurture.htm

Duley, Margaret -
Newfoundland/Labrador
Riggs, Bert. Margaret Duley Papers.
COLL -248, September, 1994;
September 1998. Centre for
Newfoundland Studies Archives,
Memorial University of
Newfoundland.

Dyck, Lillian Eva - Saskatchewan
IW Interview, Summer, 2000.

El-Tahan, Mona - Newfoundland
IW Interview, Summer, 2000.
The Express,Toronto, June, 28,
2000.
Atlantic Progress, Jan-Feb, 2000.
Canadian Business, October 30,
1998.

Moussa, Faraq. Women Inventors
Organizations. IFIA Publications
No. 1, Geneva, 1994.

Filipovic, Dusanka - Ontario
IW Interview, Summer, 2000.

Sources

Canadian Patent Database.
Toronto Star, Toronto, May, 1992.
Halifax Chronicle Herald, Halifax,
September, 1993.

Fedoruk, Sylvia - Saskatchewan
IW Interview, Summer, 2000.
Canadian Manager/Manager
Canadien - Fall, 1991.
Publication Unknown, February 4,
1957: Prizes at Bonspiel.
Publication Unknown, February
1957: Joyce McKee Four Takes
Women's Bonspiel.
Maclean's Magazine, February 15,
1952: The Atom Bomb That Saves
Lives.
Nature Magazine, 1951.
Saskatchewan News Index, June 9,
2000.
Canada Encyclopedia World CD.

Fehr, Marjorie - Saskatchewan
IW Interview, Summer, 2000.

Forchuk Skrypuch, Marsha - Ontario
IW Interview Summer, 2000.
www.calla.com/pads.html

Foster, Cyndi - Nunavut
IW Interview 2000.
Northern News Services, January
1997.
www.expertcanmore.net/earthpaper

Fraser-Jellett, Joanne - Nova Scotia
IW Interview, Summer, 2000.
The Daily News, Halifax, July 20,
1999.

Galloway, Kelly - Prince Edward
Island
IW Interview, Summer, 2000.
Engineering Technologies Canada,
pamphlet.

Gelhorn, Carolyn – Manitoba
Canadian Patent Database.
IW Interview, Summer, 2000.
Bohnert, Beth, Canadian Women Risk
Takers and Change Makers. The
Women Inventors Project, Toronto,
1993.

Gérin-Lajoie, Marie Lacoste - Quebec

Cleverdon, Catherine L., The Woman
Suffrage Movement in Canada. –
University of Toronto Press, 1973.
Dumont, Micheline, Quebec Women,
A History by the Clio Collective.
Women's Press,1987.
www.nlc-bnc.ca/digiproj/women

National Library of Canada.

Giancaspro, Giovanna - Quebec
IW Interview, Summer, 2000.
Hockey Trades, March 31, 2000.

Grannan, Mary - New Brunswick
CBC Archives www.friendscb.org/cal-
endar/2000/february.htm
New Brunswick Archives.

Greiner, Liana - British Columbia
IW Interview, Summer, 2000.
Greiner, Liana: Pine-O-Mite. Gr.7
Science Fair Project.

Hind, Ella Cora. - Manitoba
Brave Harvest: The Story of E. Cora
Hind, - LL.D . Toronto,Thomas Hind
Ltd., 1945.
Hind, E. Cora, - My Travels and
Findings. Macmillan, Toronto, 1939.

Highland Thunder Electric Racing -
Nova Scotia
IW Interview, 2001.
Industry Canada www.ic.gc.ca
The Ottawa Citizen, Ottawa, March
1998: Wheels on the Web.

Hayden, Joyce - Yukon
IW Interview, Summer, 2000.
The Yukon News, January, 1974.
Whitehorse Star, October, 1974.

Howell, Jackie - Newfoundland
IW Interview, Summer, 2000.
The Express Newspaper, May 2000.

Johnson, Madeleine - Quebec
Canadian Patent Database.

Johnson, Plum Lind - Ontario
IW Interview, Summer, 2000.
City Woman, July /August 1996.

Jubinville, Gisele - Alberta
IW Interview, Summer, 2000.

Chatelaine, November. 1993, 1995.
Canadian Industrial Innovation
Centre.
Canadian Patent Database.

Katz, Barry M., Technology and
Culture: A Historical Romance.
Stanford Alumni Association,
Stanford, 1990.

Klein, Colleen Chips - Ontario
IW Interview Summer, 2000.
Canadian Patent Database.
Bohnert, Beth , Canadian Women
Risk Takers and Change Makers. The
Women Inventors Project, Toronto,
1993.

Kumacheva, Eugenia - Ontario
IW Interview, Summer, 2000.
The Globe & Mail, Toronto, April,
2000.

Levy, Julia - British Columbia
IW Interview, Summer, 2000.
Time, November 29, 1999.
The Financial Post Magazine,
December, 1998.
Newsweek, January 26, 1998.

Levy, Sarah and Alexandra - Quebec
IW Interview, Summer, 2000.

MacDonald, Anne L., Feminine
Ingenuity : How Women Inventors
Changed America. Ballantine Books,
New York, 1992.

MacFarlane, Constance Ida - Prince
Edward Island
Seaweed Flora of the Maritimes: Irish
Moss in the Maritime Provinces.
National Research Council Canada,
1956.
Outstanding Women of PEI. Zonta
Club, Charlottetown, 1981.

MacGill, Elsie - Ontario
Toronto Star, March, 1990.
Toronto Star, October, 1985.
Cook, Sharon Ann, Framing Our Past:
Canadian Women's History in the
Twentieth Century. McGill-Queen's
University Press, 2001.

Sources

Malley, Diane - Manitoba
IW Interview, Summer, 2000.

Martin-Robichaud, Debbie - New Brunswick
IW Interview, Summer 2000.

Marais, Irene Felicite - Quebec
Canadian Patent Database.

Mathis, Nancy - New Brunswick
IW Interview, Summer, 2000.
New Brunswick Telegraph Journal, October, 1998.

Melo, Stella
IW Interview, Summer, 2000.

Michaud, Barbara - New Brunswick
IW Interview, Summer, 2000.
L'Acadie Nouvelle, Janvier, 1998.

Mignault, Lorraine - Manitoba
IW Interview, Summer, 2000.
Chatelaine, September, 1999.
The Winnipeg Sun, June, 1999.
L'Express Toronto, June, 1999.

Milner, Brenda - Quebec
Canadian Medical Hall of Fame.
www.cdnmedhall.org?Inductees/milner97.htm

Murphy, Wendy - Ontario
IW Interview, Winter, 1999.
Chatelaine, November, 1995.
Royal Bank Reporter, Fall, 1992.
The Canadian Inventors Newsletter, Spring, 1991.

Native Technology - North
McClellan, Catherine, My Old People Say: An Ethnographic Survey of Southern Yukon Territory. National Museums of Canada, 1975.

Newton, Margaret - Manitoba
www.residences.mcgill.ca/rvc/rvcthree.htm.
Canadian Science and Engineering Hall of Fame.
www.corpserv.nrc.ca/corpserv/hall/u/_io9_e.html

Novaczek, Irene - Prince Edward Island

IW Interview, Summer, 2000.
Common Ground, vol. 12, no. 3, p. 18, June 1993: Women in Support of Fishing Market Sea Plant Delicacies.

Panabaker, Janet, Inventing Women, Profiles of Women Inventors. The Women Inventors Project, 1991.

Paris-Seeley, Nancy - British Columbia
IW Interview, Summer, 2000.

Payette, Julie - Quebec
IW Interview, Winter 2001.
National Post, September 8, 1999: Payette to Help Team Canada's Image.
Toronto Star, July 14, 1999: Astronaut Leaves Her Young Fans Star-Struck.
Maclean's, June 14, 1999: Mission Accomplished for Payette.

Percival, Debra James - Prince Edward Island
IW Interview, Summer, 2000.
The Buzz, May 2000.

Perri, Sabrina, - Quebec
IW Interview, Summer, 2000.
Whitehorse Star, May 17, 1995: Student May Have Work Produced.

Petrell, Royann - British Columbia
IW Interview, Summer, 2000.

Peters, Aganetta - Manitoba
Canadian Patent Database.

Pettersen, Judy - Manitoba
IW Interview, Summer, 2000.
Canadian Living, February, 2000.
Winnipeg Sun, September 26, 1999.

Robinson, Laura - Ontario
London Magazine, February 1993.
Panabaker, Janet, Inventing Women: Profiles of Women Inventors. The Women Inventors Project, 1991.

Russell, Inge - Ontario
IW Interview 2000.
London Magazine, February 1993.
Panabaker, Janet. Inventing Women: Profiles of Women Inventors. The Women Inventors Project 1991.

Profeit-LeBlanc, Louse - Yukon
IW Interview, Summer, 2000.
www.yukoncollege.yk.ca/agra-ham/womensconf/nwotable5.htm

Schinkle, Clara - Yukon
IW Interview, Summer 2000.
www.yukoncollege.yk.ca/agra-ham/womensconf/nwotable3.htm

Simon, Sara - NWT
IW Interview, Summer, 2000.
The Globe & Mail, Toronto, date unknown.
www.yukoncollege.yk.ca/agra-ham/womensconf/nwotable3.htm
Simon, Sara: A Pictorial Account of Family, Church, and Community. Council for Yukon Indians and the Government of the Yukon.Whitehorse, 1982.

Stanley, Autumn, Mothers and Daughters of Invention : Notes for a Revised History of Technology. Rutgers University Press, New Brunswick, 1993.

Thompson, Elaine - Manitoba
IW Interview, Summer, 2000.
CBC News World, April, 1992.

Wayland Barber, Elizabeth, Women's Work : The First 20,000 Years : Women, Cloth, and Society in Early Times. W. W. Norton & Company, New York, 1994.

White, Mary Anne - Nova Scotia
IW Interview, Summer, 2000.

Zimmerman, Rachel - Ontario
IW Interview, Summer, 2000.
London Magazine, February 1993.
Canadian Mentor/Tech Ed Project: Interview August 1998.
Panabaker, Janet. Inventing Women : Profiles of Women Inventors.The Women Inventors Project 1991.